DIMENSION ONE
THE LAWS OF THE UNIVERSE ACCORDING TO TAO

MASTER WAYSUN LIAO

Copyright 2022 © Waysun Liao
Taichi Tao Productions
433 South Boulevard
Oak Park, Illinois 60302 USA
www.taichitaocenter.com

ISBN: 978-1-7366804-1-4 (Paperback)
ISBN: 978-1-7366804-0-7 (E-Book)
Cover Art by Caleb Nussear
Supercollider, 2021, ink on Shiramine paper
Design Director, Meiling Chen
Cover design by Iskon Design
All rights reserved.
Nothing in this book may be reproduced or reprinted in any form or by any means, including electronic or mechanical, photocopying or recording, without express permission of the publisher.

ACKNOWLEDGEMENTS

Taichi Tao Productions and the author would like to thank the many people who made this book possible, including our editor Tracy Litsey, our design director Meiling Chen, artist Caleb Nussear for his work appearing both on the cover and in several interior sketches, our project advisor Lincoln C. Bickford, PhD, MD, and cover designer Iskon Design Inc. We especially thank our publishing consultant Ben C. Allen and his team at Tonic Books. That team includes Erica Statly, Krista Munster, Gail Ramberg and Susan Veach.

TABLE OF CONTENTS

ACKNOWLEDGEMENTS	3
INTRODUCTION	7
PART ONE: STARTING FROM NOTHING	13
Dimensions: The More the Merrier	15
First Things First	17
Nothing: Special!	21
Understand Nothing by the Way It Works	23
DO – First Note, First Dimension	25
PART TWO: THE BELLOWS	29
Dimension One and Ultimate Truth	30
Inward and Outward, Yin and Yang	32
Something Out of Nothing	35
Our Material Bias	39
Breath and Thought: More Bellows	43
Change Is Ultimate Truth	45
The Bellows of Human Nature	46
Day Dream, Night Dream	51
PART THREE: THE ONE POWER	61
Stillness and Motion	62
Neng and Kong	63
Neng Thinks and Creates Reality	64

Kong Struggles to Return to Nothing	69
DO Is the Ability to Think!	72
Evolution or Devolution	79
The Uncarved Block	82

PART FOUR: THE NET — 89

Action, Reaction, and Heaven's Net	90
Heaven's Web, Though Invisible, is Eternal and Infinite in Its Immensity	94
Everything Is Created by the Oddness of That Web Action	100
All Actions Are Destined to Ceaseless Interactions	103
Nothing Escapes or Parts from This Invisible Web	111
DO Is Like a Gong	117

PART FIVE: DO SCIENCE — 123

Untangling the Net: The Science of DO	124
DO Science Is Multidimensional	128
Trillions of Dimensions	133
Defusing Karmic Dynamite	138
Managing Emotions	146
The Truth about Suffering	151
No Conflict, No Escape	157
You Are Your Own Dojo	163
The Goal of the Original Taoists	167

CONCLUSION — 175

PUBLISHER'S NOTE — 187

INTRODUCTION

We congratulate ourselves as the generation with the most advanced technology and greatest aggregate knowledge in human history. But are we? If we are, it's a sad state of affairs.

This book presents several outlandish propositions—one being that sages from ancient traditions, such as Taoism, may have known more about the universe than we do now. We explore whether their understanding of physics, the human mind, the mechanics of time, and the unfolding of human history could have been much deeper than ours.

It's hard for modern minds to accept that a quirky old relic like Taoism might hold insight that can broaden our understanding of science, humanities, and psychology today. It's even harder to believe that their discoveries could steer our technology and society back on a course that could prolong our survival as a species rather than our current collective self-destruction.

Taoism is layered with complex cultural and religious interpretations, allegories, and symbolism. When you first try and understand the concept of Tao, it defies common sense. Even seasoned scholars still scratch their heads, wondering whether they really know what all those complicated old Taoist scrolls and books are talking about. They talk of Yin and Yang, ovens and crucibles, black pearls and yellow shoots, and the power of the void.

Whether it's mysterious and arcane instructions, elixirs of immortality, or advice on spiritual alchemy in the Taoist canon, we have a hard time understanding what those ancient Chinese monks and masters were trying to teach us. This is by design. Due to competition between different Taoist temples and sects and not wanting to share their knowledge with outsiders, old Taoist masters hid their wisdom in what appears like secret code.

Those crafty old Taoists used those strange words to lock up what they knew from prying snoops like you and me. If you only have those books and scrolls, it's impossible to make sense of it all. You need the verbal decoding of a master—in other words, the oral teachings passed down from "mouth to ear"—to unlock the wisdom. Those verbal teachings are the deciphering key.

When you have that "mouth-to-ear" key and unlock the code, that old Taoist wisdom is no different than the latest findings and most brilliant theories coming from today's modern scientists. Those funny words and Taoist codes were just the language they used to report their discoveries.

Those ancient Taoists described the same powers we observe when we split atoms in an accelerator or track cellular regeneration under a microscope. Without X-rays or televisions or radioactive isotopes, they understood the penetrating power of invisible energy waves. Without satellites or telescopes, the ancient Taoists accurately described attributes of faraway galaxies and stars and even the very boundaries of the universe.

In addition to locking their truth in a box made of codes and symbols, Taoist teachings were also hidden by layers of cultural and academic misinterpretation. It's as if that box was locked inside another box, inside another box, and then a larger box, then locked inside a giant warehouse called "eastern philosophies."

Tao teachings, like those of Lao Tzu in his *Tao Te Ching*, became part of China's philosophical and cultural fabric for centuries up through today. Unfortunately, they were diluted and chopped up into everyday platitudes, superstitions, and household wisdom. Along the way, their commonplace applications blurred the larger Taoist roadmap to universal truths.

Many in both the Eastern and Western hemispheres embraced the teachings of Lao Tzu and his "Tao" as a guide for balance, moderation, simplicity, and a return to a more natural way of life. They literally loved it to death with an avalanche of new translations and commentaries. While these helped preserve the *Tao Te Ching*'s popularity, they left today's understanding of Lao Tzu's truth more like a watered-down virgin cocktail. It carries enough flavor of Taoism to satisfy your taste but little of the true punch and power of its original recipe.

The first references to "Tao" show up in ancient history several centuries before the birth of Christ and even before Lao Tzu himself. The original Taoist sages were mostly reclusive mystics, living far away from organized society. They were referred to as "shan ren" or "mountain men." They tended to live on their own or in small isolated communities, where they could carry on with their meditations and live closer to nature.

These mountain men combined their immense wisdom on energy and the universe with advice on how to live a better life and avoid conflict or troubles. They tried to describe what would happen to people after their death and what lay beyond our human world. The plethora of lifestyle guidelines and tales of the afterlife are why many later scholars interpreted Tao wisdom in religious terms. The original teaching of Taoism was never designed as a formalized religion. It only became formalized over time through misplaced enthusiasm and human error.

The earliest Taoist sects had one foot in Tao wisdom and another in more primitive local superstitions. You can trace the evolution of different branches of Taoism to different regional beliefs. You can also trace the influence of other religions or political movements prevailing in those regions, such as Confucianism, Mohism, or Buddhism. Some sects even worshipped Lao Tzu as a god, although he never claimed to be one.

So, what is the study of Tao really? Is it about science, philosophy, or religion? We are forced to limit it by such categories since we always try to put this wisdom into words. The answer is that it's all of these and yet none of these.

To get to the root of Tao and what it is, we have to tear open and toss aside all the nesting boxes. That includes the boxes of cultural, religious, and philosophical interpretation, as well as the manufactured histories surrounding Taoist teaching. Once we've taken all the larger boxes away and are left with only the smallest box of pure Taoist truth, we find that it's all condensed in that small book left to us by Lao Tzu—the *Tao Te Ching*. Even so, we need the key from the "mouth-to-ear" teachings passed down through the lineage of Taoist masters through the centuries to unlock its treasures.

Introduction

When we open the treasure box so its jewels can shine, we find that Tao wisdom holds true whether we are talking about science, philosophy, religion, sociology, mathematics, love, war, outer space, or the struggles of our daily lives. They are universal, infinite, and immutable.

Those immutable truths that Taoists discovered are what this book is made of. With this book, you'll be able to decode so much more in the *Tao Te Ching* and also decode more about our world while you are walking in nature, exploring science, examining history, staring at a starry sky, or swapping tales at the corner barbershop.

The lessons of Tao can also help you navigate the ups and downs of your personal life. How? By explaining what has confused so many for so long: why, despite our best efforts, we cannot individually or collectively seem to pull ourselves out of suffering. Through understanding why suffering is inevitable and what causes it, you can employ the laws of the universe to reduce your distress and start on a path of more effective living.

The best part about this book is that when people ask you, "Hey, what the heck is that book you are reading all about? Is it science fiction? A religious book? A new look at physics?" you can just laugh and tell them, "This book? It's nothing!" Then you'll be exactly like those crafty old masters, keeping this ultimate secret from them by telling them the absolute truth and thereby hiding it in plain sight, just like a real Taoist!

See, that's what this book's all about—*it's about nothing!*

PART ONE

STARTING FROM NOTHING

*"Look, but you cannot see it—it is formless.
Listen, but you cannot hear it—it transcends sound.
Grasp, but you can hold nothing—it is intangible.
These three are unfathomable; therefore,
they are merged as one."*

Tao Te Ching, Chapter 14

DIMENSIONS: THE MORE THE MERRIER

Have you ever been to a 3D movie? A 3D movie is special because the picture has depth—the characters and action seem to jump right out at you. It delivers a richer, more life-like experience than a simple two-dimensional film, even though both are shown on a flat screen. Ask any kid and they'll tell you a 3D movie is much more fun!

Three dimensions are not only more exciting than two; more dimensions give us more information and a fuller understanding of an object.

If you had never seen a cow in your life, what would give you the best understanding of a cow? A photo of a cow? A movie of cows in a pasture? Better yet, how about a Guernsey cow in your living room? The more dimensions you add to the experience, the better you understand the term "cow."

In our lives, most of us are trying to add dimensions to our experience. We feel that more of anything and everything enhances our lives, broadening our understanding and enjoyment. We want more colors, more sounds, more flavors, more friends, more travel, more technology. Most people's top goals are to gain more money, more power, more education, more titles, more health, etc. Our whole society seems to be built around the pursuit of more.

If you compare our modern-day life with the typical life people lived only 300 years ago, we have many more dimensions of experience available to us than we could have even imagined back then. Think about life before the Industrial Revolution. We spent countless centuries living much the same way—in little kingdoms as merchants and farmers with maybe a few horses or a wagon to carry us around.

Then came the steam engine, electricity, the telephone, the automobile, the airplane, computers, space travel, and so much more! It's as if the dimensions of what we could do, know, and explore exploded exponentially!

But there is one problem: As we add more dimensions, we also add more complication to our lives. Due to this rising complexity, many of us feel too busy, exhausted, overwhelmed, out of touch, disoriented, and overstimulated.

Deep inside, we somehow sense that while we've gained so much with the explosion of human endeavor, we are also at risk of losing something very important. We can't always name it—but the wider our sphere of influence becomes, there is a nameless hole in our being that grows along with it. That is why there is also a contemporary movement to simplify our lifestyles, to slow down, get back to nature, and stop scrambling for more.

Some of us are starting to wake up and realize that more stimulation, more information, and being busy all the time can *detract* from our experience and understanding of life. We're tired of feeling constantly distracted from what's important and what is real. We want to get back to the basics and the root of human life—whatever that is, and wherever we lost it.

If expanding our experience broadens our minds and understanding, but simplifying our lives preserves our

PART ONE: Starting from Nothing 17

sense of wholeness and connection to what's real, which way is the best way to go? Should we be reaching out for more layers to our experience or simplify our focus on something more primary? Do added dimensions deliver more truth? Or do they make everything more complicated and confusing?

Let's look at what we refer to as "dimensions" on our journey so that we can find the answer.

FIRST THINGS FIRST

In grade school math, we study three dimensions: height, width, and depth. Scientists believe there are more than just three. Some say that time is its own dimension. Physicists argue for 10, 11, or 26 dimensions. A few scientists and science fiction authors even believe in parallel worlds and that these parallel dimensions are folded into the very space we walk around in every day.

It's tough for us to nail down how many dimensions there are and what they are like because we seem to be firmly stuck in our own dimension of space, time, and matter. Yet that doesn't diminish the excitement and mystery of imagining the possibilities of a multidimensional world.

But wait a minute. Here is a question that nobody seems to ask: What is the *first* dimension? *Dimension One?*

When you strip all the other dimensions down, whether they are imaginary, theoretical, or real, and start taking away the basic dimensions of height, width, and depth, where is the primary dimension from which they were all built? Which is the first?

Let's see what we can find by taking apart the three dimensions we all are familiar with.

A cube has three dimensions: height, width, and depth. If we strip down a three-dimensional cube, it's built from six two-dimensional squares. We say they are two-dimensional because they have height and width. You can't build a three-dimensional cube without the two-dimensional squares.

PART ONE: Starting from Nothing

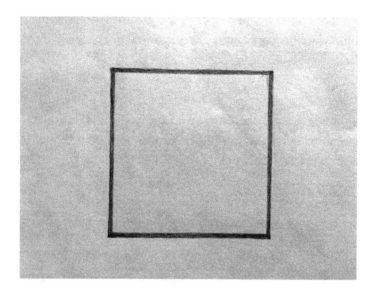

Each of these squares can be broken down further into four simple two-dimensional lines. The lines are also two-dimensional because they have height and width. You can't build the square without those lines.

So we can break a cube down into squares and lines, but what do those squares and lines break down into? Where is the first dimension?

We know that we can break down any line into a string of points. It's a point that's the starting place from which we begin to draw the very first line of a square, circle, rectangle, or any other two-dimensional shape. It always starts with a point.

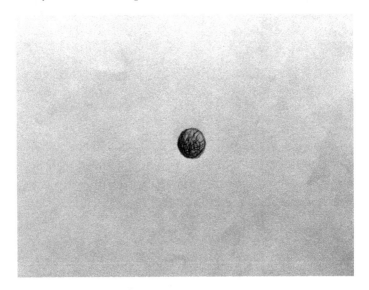

Anything you touch is a point in space. Space is made up of an infinite number of points. Even when we examine time, we always start with a "point in time." So is a point the first dimension? Dimension One?

Well, we are getting closer. But the small point above on this paper still has height, width, and depth when we measure that tiny drop of ink. Even if we broke down that ink drop into sub-points or even sub-atomic particles, we could still theoretically measure their dimensions. If we

PART ONE: Starting from Nothing

can still measure height, depth, width on any scale, no matter how small, we are still locked in a two or three-dimensional landscape—we would still fall short of finding Dimension One.

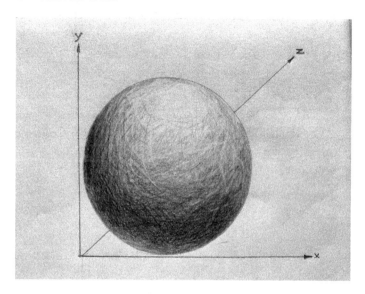

NOTHING: SPECIAL!

If we keep breaking one point down, going deeper into the center of that point, theoretically, we'd eventually reach nothingness—the place where there is no longer anything to measure. That would be true of any point in space or time we choose. *Nothingness is the ultimate destination as we go further into any point.*

Believe it or not, *it is that very nothingness that is the first dimension!* It's the center of a point, existing at the place where the point becomes nothing. That place has no height, width, or depth. *Dimension One is nothing!*

This nothingness is very special. It is the origin of everything. Out of this nothing springs the entire universe. It is the foundation of every other dimension, the root of all phenomena. No matter what dimension you study or find yourself in, you'll find it is made from nothing because it has Dimension One as its foundation.

The other attribute of nothingness is it's everywhere. The chair you sit in and the table where you eat dinner are made up of molecules comprised mostly of emptiness. If you could examine your chair with an electron microscope, you'd see pretty quickly that between each atom and between the whirling protons and electrons within each atom is a proportionally vast field of nothing. If you knew how much emptiness made up the chair you are sitting in, you'd wonder how it could ever hold you up!

Space, too, is a field of mostly nothing. We look up into the night sky and see billions of stars. But if you were to condense all those twinkling lights of matter together, you would have far more emptiness than "star."

Just about everything we think of as solid has emptiness flowing in and out of it: Every atom, every sub-atomic particle, all of them whirl in a sea of nothing.

Emptiness is the vast sea that flows between every sub-particle of every atom. Because of this, emptiness is the only one "substance" that is always continually connected to itself. Since it is always connected to itself (in a way that no piece of "matter" could ever be), it is one unified piece—one fabric extending throughout the entire universe.

Since nothingness is connected and one piece

spanning everywhere in all dimensions, it is infinitely big. Since it is also indivisible into smaller parts, being "smaller" than the smallest sub-atomic particle, it is also infinitely small.

Everywhere, indivisible, one-piece, infinitely large yet infinitely small—only nothingness qualifies as a candidate for the title of first dimension!

UNDERSTAND NOTHING BY THE WAY IT WORKS

It's difficult to accept nothingness as a dimension. We don't have any sensors to detect nothingness. In fact, we judge nothingness as the *absence* of what can stimulate our senses. We rely on the contrast of stimulation in order to know that we feel nothing.

Since we judge nothing based on our limited senses, sometimes we think we're surrounded by nothingness, but it's not true. Just because we don't detect anything doesn't mean there's nothing there.

For example, we can sit in an empty room and hear nothing, see nothing, smell nothing. But a dog could detect all sorts of information from sounds and smells in the room that our limited senses can't. So even when we think we know what nothingness is, we can't really be sure that what we judge as emptiness is truly empty. It may actually be full of information or substances we can't detect. In the same way, we never think about the air around us because it is invisible. But when the wind blows our hat off, or when we swallow something the wrong way and are coughing and gasping for breath, we clearly understand that air has substance and is far from nothing.

The dimension of nothingness we are talking about is not like "air" or invisible smells and sounds. The first dimension is pure emptiness.

We are always right in the midst of that emptiness, and that same emptiness is within and around every particle of our being. It follows us wherever we go—in, out, and throughout our bodies.

This creates a problem. The problem is that since we can never be outside of the first dimension, we can never observe it from a detached position. For this reason, we have no real means to study it or even detect what it's doing. We are like fish in a lake trying to understand the water.

The only way a fish might learn to feel or know it is surrounded by water is if that water starts to move. It might be able to sense that water moving against its body, or it might observe the water's movement having the effect of pushing the seaweed back and forth or pushing other creatures to and fro.

Like those fish in the moving water, although we cannot directly perceive nothingness, we can look around us for clues to how this nothingness works. Just as we can't see the invisible wind, we can know which way it is blowing by the way it blows the leaves on the trees or a windsock.

Similarly, we can see the effects of the first dimension, nothingness, by observing its effects on everything else. Even though we can't observe it directly, we can learn about it by watching the *way* it works.

DO – FIRST NOTE, FIRST DIMENSION

A Taoist's main pursuit is to understand Tao. What is Tao? The word means "the way." This is why an ancient Chinese wise man named Lao Tzu used the word "Tao" or the "Way" to describe this original nothingness. Lao Tzu described it as the "way" since we can't see the invisible nothingness of Dimension One and can only understand it by watching the *way* it works—the effect it has on what we *can* see and experience. His book, the *Tao Te Ching*, is like his collection of lab notes where he wrote down his observations on the way this invisible power of the universe works. Lao Tzu was the first scientist, the first pioneer, to research and report his contact with the first dimension.

Lao Tzu wasn't the first to coin the term "Tao." In ancient Chinese, the word Tao (pronounced "Dow") is derived from an even older word: "Do." This Do is pronounced like the same "Do" that is the first note on our musical scale, or like the dough of a pastry chef. Both Tao and Do mean "way."

道 = Tao or Do

Although in China they use the word Tao, in other parts of Asia, like Japan, they still use the older version Do. For example, in Japan, you'll find a religion called "Shin Do," meaning "spirit way," or a martial art called "Ju Do," meaning "soft way."

For us, what is most useful about the word Do is that it conveniently serves as our abbreviation in this book for Dimension One—"D.O." So while we explore the fascinating power and explosive potential of the first dimension, we'll save time and call it "DO."

Why bother learning about the first dimension—DO?

If DO is the root and foundation of all the other dimensions, then understanding it may be the most important scientific, intellectual, and spiritual task of all! Whether you are in dimension 2, 3, 6, 26, or dimension 10,000, they all have Dimension One as their starting point and building block. It's woven into everything. Once you understand DO, it's like pulling the edge of a string that unravels the whole fabric. It's the master code to the entire universe!

The science of DO can help you understand everything better—whether it be the wonders of the universe, our human world and its challenges, or even how to manage your own life more effectively.

Philosophers, religious teachers, astronomers, and physicists have all bumped into the same laws of DO. They each explained them differently based on the narrow limits of their specialized discipline. They are like the four blind men describing an elephant. The man who held its tail described an elephant like a rope; the one who held its leg described it as a tree trunk; the one who held the ear described it as a heavy woolen blanket, and the one who held the trunk described it as a giant snake. They were all feeling the same animal but experiencing it differently depending on which piece they felt.

So today, we have scientists, philosophers, and religious leaders arguing or competing with each other to describe the truth of the universe. If they all could see the bigger picture of Dimension One, they would understand that they are trying to explain the same reality, same laws, same experience—the same elephant—and don't even know it!

In this book, we won't just talk about this mysterious Dimension One. We'll actually hold the tail, the ear, the leg, and the trunk, and then we will learn how to take our blindfolds off so that we can experience the entire elephant. After we see the whole elephant, we'll hop on and ride it home. We will step off the pages of this book, beyond imagination and intellect, and dive into the very root of consciousness and existence.

Are you ready to explore a whole new dimension? One you've been living in all along but could never even see or imagine? Let's go!

PART TWO

THE BELLOWS

*"Isn't the space between heaven and earth like a bellows?
The more the empty space, the more it offers.
The more it moves, the more it generates."*

Tao Te Ching, Chapter 5

DIMENSION ONE AND ULTIMATE TRUTH

The reason understanding Dimension One is so critical is that if we can grasp even a little about how it works, we have the key to ultimate truth. Why? Since DO is the foundation for all other dimensions, its nature will remain constant through all of them, giving us valuable understanding of every part of our universe. It would finally provide that universal measuring stick, a unifying theorem of sorts, to help us understand virtually everything.

To qualify as an ultimate truth, the conclusions we make about the nature of Dimension One cannot change—ever. Ultimate truth, doesn't change if you go from Chicago to London. It's not like the truth we obey when we all agree we should drive on the right side of the road here in the United States. If we travel to England, that so-called "truth" changes, and we drive on the left. Ultimate truth must be a universal law in *every* case, not just here or there or when we all manage to agree on it.

Finding a universal truth is hard. Even the basic building blocks of our reality are not necessarily universal truths. Let's take a piece of reality that we live with every day: time. Is time an ultimate truth? Albert Einstein pointed out that time changes when we leave the planet. In fact, this discrepancy in how time behaves in space versus on Earth requires us to program satellites to compensate for those differences. If we don't make those compensations, our GPS instruments can't function properly here on Earth.

Likewise, Einstein showed that not only does time change in space, but "space" itself can bend. He proved

Part Two: The Bellows

that light traveling at a far distance seems to bend around objects—meaning the *space* carrying the beam of light is what *bends*, not the light.

If time and space can bend and change from one setting to another, then neither can be an ultimate truth, and neither time nor space can be Dimension One. Dimension One must be *more original* and fundamental than even time or space. It means the laws of Dimension One will always apply to time and space, but the laws of time and space do not always apply to DO.

This is why DO is primary to time and space, a foundation underlying time and space, more basic and fundamental—*more "true."* When I use the word true in this instance, I'm using it the way a carpenter or architect would.

When we want to line a board or brick perfectly perpendicular or parallel to a wall, we "true" it by comparing it to another reference that we know for certain is perfectly aligned—like a plumb line or a level. Since DO is more true than time or space, we know we can now use DO as our plumb and level to understand time and space but not the other way around. Time and space can change, so they are poor and unreliable levels. They are not "true."

When we can find a level, plumb line, or ruler that is truer than time and space and is found in everything, everywhere, that's pretty powerful! Lao Tzu puts it this way: *"Even though it is minute* (very small, invisible, like nothingness), *nothing can dominate it* (because it is primary and wields ultimate truth over all other dimensions)."

Lao Tzu describes Dimension One as *"Bu Xiao."* In Chinese, that means there is "nothing like it." The reason there is nothing like DO is that DO cannot be increased, divided, annihilated, improved, or changed. Think about it: Can you increase nothingness, divide nothingness, annihilate nothingness, improve or change nothingness? No! With these unique and important traits of Bu Xiao, nothingness or DO is automatically in the category of universal truth.

INWARD AND OUTWARD, YIN AND YANG

Here is one ultimate truth about Dimension One: The old Taoists believed that within Dimension One are two conjoined forces that make the whole universe possible—Yin and Yang.

Yin and Yang can seem like mysterious Asian terms, and they have been used in many confusing ways over the years. For our purposes, we are going to say that they simply mean the forces of inward and outward. Yin is a force pulling inward, and Yang a force pushing outward.

What Lao Tzu discovered was that *Dimension One is the origin of both Yin and Yang and simultaneously has and wields both inward and outward power.* As the primary forces of DO, inward and outward create the framework, the warp and woof of the entire fabric of the universe. Think of them as two steel girders holding up a skyscraper, but in this case, these two girders hold up all of existence.

Yin and Yang are like inseparable sister and brother. They are two sides of the same coin and always come together in one package. You will never find one without the other. Both an inward and outward force of energy are necessary for all things to exist. They make structure possible. Without some sort of inward force, everything would fly apart. Without some sort of outward energy, everything would collapse in upon itself.

If this apple I hold in my hand had only outward Yang force but had no Yin force holding its molecules together, it would instantly vaporize into dust and disappear into thin air. But if my apple had *only* inward or Yin force without the balancing outward force of Yang, its molecules would pull inward until it became a tiny particle so dense that it would fall through a hole in my hand and down through the Earth. My apple needs both an inward and outward force to maintain its shape and exist as my delicious snack.

This isn't only true of solid objects but everything we know. Without Yin force acting on our atmosphere, our air, including all of our vital oxygen, would fly outward into infinity, making life on Earth impossible. But without some sort of outward Yang force keeping its molecules apart, the air would condense and become far too thick for survival. It would ultimately collapse into a solid rather than its life-sustaining gaseous state. Air has a perfect balance of both Yin and Yang to sustain its life-giving nature for beings that breathe.

Pure exclusive Yang can never exist because it would expand so completely and swiftly with nothing to keep it in check that it would leave in its wake an expanding and total vacuum. Pure exclusive Yin can never exist because it would instantly create one super-dense mass that sucked the entire universe inside of it. You will always find Yin and Yang together. There is no exception.

With these examples, you can see what those Tao masters were trying to teach us when they said everything is made out of Yin and Yang: Everything must have both an inward and outward force in order to exist. It must have "inward" to hold it together and "outward" to have presence and sustain itself. It's a universal law that applies to everything under every circumstance: From the subatomic level to the molecular level to the largest galaxies in the universe, everything exists because of the complicated play between the two forces of inward and outward.

Let's look at one of the biggest and most powerful objects in our lives—the Sun. The Sun is a perfect example of how both inward power and outward power can balance and work together. We rely on the immense inward force of our Sun's gravity to hold our solar system together. Gravity is the Sun's "Yin" force. At the same time, where would we be without the outward radiance of the Sun to give us heat and light? The heat and light radiating from the Sun is its "Yang" force.

If the Sun's inward force was even a fraction greater than it is now, our planet couldn't exist. Gravity would suck our Earth into the Sun's surface or at least pull our planet much too close for it to sustain life. If the Sun's outward force were any greater, the heat and radiation would destroy life on our planet, and the Sun would burn itself out very quickly or explode altogether.

The primary principles of inward and outward are not just found in our physical universe; they are the rudimentary building blocks that sustain life itself. We have the forces of Yin and Yang in our own bodies: We inhale and exhale, drink and perspire, eat and eliminate, in a constant flow of inward and outward that sustains our very life. If one force takes over, our health quickly deteriorates. Imagine if you could drink and drink and drink but could never urinate or perspire. How long would you live? Or how about if you could only exhale but never inhale?

All life forms we know of, from the cellular level on up, rely on the power of inward and outward to survive and keep in balance. Dimension One, the original building block of the universe, is the source of that inward and outward force.

So now we have a second universal truth held within DO: The combined inward and outward potential within nothingness is the backbone of our universe, giving everything structure, existence, and even the ability to sustain life.

Let's explore more about this universal principle of inward and outward to discover more about DO.

SOMETHING OUT OF NOTHING

If we are saying that inward and outward are a universal truth—a truth that exists inside Dimension One—what we're really saying is that *what we call nothing is moving*! Can nothingness move?

Lao Tzu says, "Yes! DO moves inward and outward like a bellows."

"Isn't the space between heaven and earth like a bellows?
The more the empty space, the more it offers.
The more it moves, the more it generates."

Tao Te Ching, Chapter 5

A bellows is an old-fashioned air pump used to fan a flame. It pulls air in and then pushes it out. It's a perfect representation of Yin and Yang, inward and outward, providing a tool for understanding how DO works and how it moves.

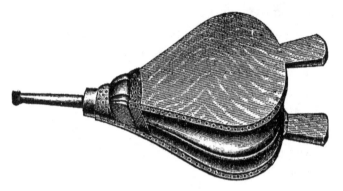

In order for a bellows to create wind and do its job, it has to move. If a bellows doesn't move, nothing happens. Likewise, if Dimension One didn't move—didn't possess and wield that inward and outward force, nothing would happen. Literally, nothing would exist.

But thank goodness DO is continually pumping that universal inward and outward force, generating everything everywhere in all possible dimensions.

How can this bellows motion create the entire universe out of nothing? Let's explore this bellows power by going down to the smallest possible building blocks of our material world: *sub-atomic particles*.

Scientists keep finding and classifying newer and smaller particles on their quest to find the one magical particle that will explain how all the others work. They believe if they could just find the *one* particle that coordinates and organizes the behavior of all the others, they will have the secret of creation at their fingertips. They call this elusive particle the "God particle."

The problem is that there is no such thing as a particle. Scientists are finding out that when you break those atoms and particles apart, there is nothing "material" there at all! All they seem to find is different patterns of energy combined with emptiness. What we call solid, material, or physical is actually a whole bunch of emptiness pulled tightly together through that inward power.

Also, the energetic reality of sub-atomic particles makes them tricky to understand since no particle is ever truly stable. They are always moving around, and their activity in this dimension is ever-changing. We have this dream of finding, naming, and examining all the many sub-atomic particles that make up our world. But what we discover is that when we want to get particles to stay still for just a moment so that we can draw conclusions about them and see what they're made of, their constitutions are too wobbly. They never seem to stop moving and changing.

The deeper we drill, we find that particles are formed by yet smaller particles—usually just bits of energy. When we talk about the smallest particles that we know of, those particles have a life that is so short that it is almost too short to even observe. It will blink and come into existence, then blink out of existence. It appears and disappears so fast that by the time we grab it or observe it, it's already changed.

When those particles disappear, we don't know where they go. They don't exist in this dimension anymore. It's as if they dissolve back into nothingness. If all they did was disappear, it would be easier to understand. But then, all of a sudden, some of them seemingly pop back into being from nothing!

It's even more confounding since those blinking particles that come and go aren't even stable as they blink in and out of our reality. A given particle doesn't blink 1-1-1-1. It blinks and changes from particle $a1$ to become a new particle $a2$, then $a3$, then $a4$. By the time I am able to grab it on the fourth blink, it has already blinked again and become particle iteration $a5$. Even as particles appear and disappear, they are constantly in a state of change.

While we watch this blinking particle wonderland, we are watching the miraculous bellows power within the emptiness. It is continually pulling in and pushing back out all the little particles of our world, huffing and puffing, inward and outward at the most microscopic levels. *Our nothingness is materializing and dematerializing subatomic particles everywhere at a fantastic rate in amazing, confounding ways!*

Scientists are so mesmerized by the nature of the particles themselves and how they change that they never stop to consider: "What is powering that bellows? What makes those particles blink in and out, appear and disappear? Where do they go?"

They miss the big picture that this little bellows pumps out a dynamic rhythm of inward and outward, alternating between "something" and "nothing" countless times in a billionth of a second. Because particles are constantly disappearing and reappearing, it's as if this bellows mechanism continually creates and annihilates matter at the same time. It is as if it writes and erases simultaneously. With particles appearing and disappearing so fast, *what we consider reality is just a flickering between something and nothing going on all around us at all times.*

Of course, the irony is that scientists who investigate subatomic particles have this same dance of particles and emptiness going on inside of them. That bellows pumping out and sucking in those flickering particles also fuels their very smart minds.

If the scientists could back up and see the bigger picture of particle activity like we are discussing today, instead of insisting on finding a so-called "God" particle to define the primary principle of the universe, they would realize that they are staring right at the real answer: *the bellows itself!*

The unifying principle scientists are looking for is not a particle but that bellows power that keeps pumping the sub-atomic building blocks of matter inward and outward from itself to create our world. That power is part and parcel of the nothingness that they throw away in their evaluation. *The signature of Dimension One is this inward-outward action potential within the emptiness itself.*

OUR MATERIAL BIAS

This true nature of the particle world—how it flickers between something and nothing in an endless dance of particles pulsing in and out from the emptiness—is the best evidence for something and nothing ultimately being the same thing and springing from the same source.

For centuries, we've all scratched our heads when we hear Eastern religions declare that something and nothing are the very same thing. Lao Tzu said it this way:

*"Always observe from formless viewpoint,
then one can see the wonderful changes.
Always observe from the viewpoint of forms,
so one can see the manifestation.
Both, though differing in name,
are made of the same source."*

Tao Te Ching, Chapter 1

*"Everything under heaven is created having forms.
Forms created from the formless."*

Tao Te Ching, Chapter 40

    It's very hard for us to believe that nothingness can hold such power. To learn that the foundation of all that exists is based in nothing makes us quite insecure. We'd rather think there was a magic particle that could explain everything. Since we are material beings ourselves, we tend to favor a more material view of the universe. It makes us feel more comfortable to think the foundation of life is solid and substantial, like a particle.

    But our material bias is based in illusion. The fact that we can see and touch matter at all is only because *the winking and blinking particles are moving so fast that they create a sensation of solidity*. That sensation is more like a movie. In a movie, thousands of small, still pictures are moving and flickering so quickly, they give the illusion of continuity. Likewise, material reality is very much like that movie. The chair you are sitting in is only giving you an illusion of cohesion and continuity. You're actually sitting on a "surface" created by the rapid movement of atoms, energy, and sub-atomic particles flickering in and out of nothing. The same goes for the material sense you have of your own body.

Let say you filled the bottom of a box with just a single layer of ping-pong balls that moved up and down very quickly—a thousand times per second. When you looked at the top of the box, it would appear solid. You could even rest your hand on it or lay a book on top of it because the rapid oscillation of the ping-pong balls would create the illusion of a solid surface. Yet the truth would be that the box was mostly empty.

Lao Tzu's *Tao Te Ching* described Taoist masters as "watchful, as if crossing a winter's stream" and "yielding, like ice about to melt." It's as if these old masters knew that the appearance of the physical world around them, including their own bodies, was more like ice about to melt—fluid, inconstant, dreamlike, suspended between substantial and insubstantial.

We like to think in material terms because it gives us a sense of security. We like to feel we can trust our physical environment as relatively constant. But is it?

This desk I am sitting at right now is not the same desk that it was one-billionth of a second ago. The molecules, atoms, and sub-atomic particles have changed so many times, in so many ways, that we can't even begin to estimate how many changes have occurred in this desk in just the last second. If I told my students my desk is not the same desk as yesterday, they would argue with me that it is. Even knowing and understanding it's just a flickering collection of changing particles, I, too, still go through my day telling myself this is the same desk I bought 30 years ago.

But my desk isn't as solid and consistent in its nature as I assume it to be. If we had the ability to completely stop those particles from blinking, that desk would disappear and return back into "nothingness." My material bias about my desk is just whistling in the dark.

When we understand the real composition of matter as the ultra-rapid motion of particles both in space as well as in and out of nothingness, DO becomes the critical "movie projector" that keeps the dance of particles and material reality seem solid and relatively constant. And thanks to the projector, we are completely engrossed in our movie.

Thanks to what we've learned about the bellows power in DO, we can now understand that *nothing is the very root of something*. Something and nothing are interchangeable and mutually depend upon each other to exist. Since the origin of something and nothing comes from within the bellows power of nothingness, this bellows is the building block of every other dimension, both material and invisible.

"All things are created from the Tao.
They are nourished by the Te.
They are formed into matter.
They are shaped by opposite powers."

Tao Te Ching, Chapter 51

Our material bias is faulty, which is why we cannot always trust what we see and what we think we know about the world. But we can implicitly trust in the bellows power of nothingness every second of every day in everything we do. We have faith that the movie will continue to play, that the flicker of reality will carry on from one moment to the next. We sit on chairs at desks and eat apples with zero worry. There is no place, no time, no occasion when we don't take for granted this bellows power.

BREATH AND THOUGHT: MORE BELLOWS

Many meditation techniques try to put us in touch with this truth of the bellows nature of DO. How? By having us focus on our own bellows power—our breathing.

In the simplest form of meditation, you can simply get quiet and watch, or better yet, feel your inhale and exhale. This can be instantly relaxing and centering, and it's a great habit to cultivate.

Most meditation that incorporates breathing can also take you all the way to an awareness of DO, where that bellows comes from, that origin of in and out. How? By continued breathing meditation, you eventually realize that the ultimate truth of the breath is that it's not the breath itself, or the air, or the oxygen that's central to life energy. It's the power that makes that bellows work. When you watch the breath long enough, you start to focus not just on the inhale and exhale but on those points in between. You watch the apex of the inhale and how it silently and reliably turns like a wheel into an exhale. And when you reach the end of the exhale, at some elusive point, the whole breathing mechanism turns to inhale once more. The power is not the inhale or exhale but the point at nothingness where that bellows mechanism keeps turning the breathing cycle over and over, whether we are awake, sleeping, conscious, or unconscious. *It's not our breath but our innate ability to breathe—it's in the mechanism where the truth lies.*

And it's not just the rhythmic in and out of our lungs and diaphragm that make up the miraculous mechanism of breathing. When we breathe in, our body absorbs particles of oxygen and other elements from the air through the membranes of the sacs in our lungs and into our bloodstream. When we breathe out, unwanted particles like carbon dioxide flow out from our bloodstream via those same sacs as a waste product we exhale. So each one of those sacs in our lungs is its own small bellows.

When the oxygen in the air we breathe enters our bloodstream, it's carried to cells that need it to sustain energy and life. That oxygen is absorbed *inward* into the cellular membrane; at the same time, cellular waste products are excreted *outward* from the cellular membrane into the blood. Then the blood carries the waste back to the lungs or to the kidney or liver to eliminate. When we meditate on the kidney and liver, we find more bellows action of absorption and excretion that helps keep us alive. Virtually every living tissue in our body functions with some variation of both inward and outward bellows power to do its job.

The same is true with our thinking. When we watch our mind carefully, we can see that the mind is like a bellows too. Thoughts come and go, seemingly in and out of nowhere, all day long. They even come and go while we sleep in the form of dreams. Our mind activity never seems to stop. But the miracle of our mind isn't in the myriad of individual thoughts themselves but rather that mechanism of conscious awareness that makes them come and go, that makes our mind activity possible. It's our ability to think—the bellows action, not our thoughts—that is the critical feature defining our intelligence.

We can look around and see that inward-outward cycle everywhere: The Sun rises and sets, summer flows into winter and then back into summer again, we are born and die. In actuality, we die every day when we go to sleep, and then we wake up again in the morning. Everywhere we look, we can see and contemplate how we are part of that grand alternation of inward and outward in our lives in everything we do.

CHANGE IS ULTIMATE TRUTH

The insight of the bellows is critical to understanding universal truth. Why? We must be careful what we call truth, nail down as fact, or try to fix into a theory, dogma, or even a book like this. Why? Because truth is a living and changing thing, always moving, just like that bellows.

Think about it: the molecules in our chair are always spinning and changing, the subatomic particles of our entire material reality are winking and blinking in and out of existence, our thoughts are rising up from nowhere and disappearing into nowhere with or without our direction. Everything is in constant motion, and yet we expect to find and nail down the truth about life and the universe in an unchanging formula that we can all understand.

The backbone of the scientific method is that a conclusion can only be made if an experiment and its results are repeatable. Yet the truth about our changing reality is that nothing is truly repeatable. Everything is in one of three states: before change, during change, or after change. We can only make predictions on observations of how and why things change.

That's why Lao Tzu chose the word *Tao* or *the Way* to describe the truth about the universe. A way is a path or process from one place to the next, one state to the next. Inherent in the word *way* is the means to make something change. Defining the ultimate truth as the "way" already lets us know that we can never pin it down in a concrete manner. We can only observe and describe it in motion by the *way* it operates, the *way* it moves, the *way* it changes.

In fact, Lao Tzu's book, the *Tao Te Ching*, is just that—a scientific notebook of observations about DO and the way the universe changes, and how we can better adapt ourselves and our world to manage those changes and employ them to our advantage rather than to our ruin.

THE BELLOWS OF HUMAN NATURE

As physical beings, we humans are bound to the forces of inward and outward too: our eyes blink; our hearts beat "ba-boom, ba-boom;" we breathe in and out; we drink and perspire; we eat and defecate; we sleep and awaken. The forces of inward and outward can be found from the cellular level on up to human reproduction.

But what many don't realize is that *this seesaw of inward and outward forces dominates us entirely*, even in our psychological makeup, our emotions, and the way our minds view the world.

In order to create a human physical form, the first primary power in the embryo is Yin, or "inward power." This "sucking power"—the power of pulling inward, accumulating and amassing together—pulled in the physical materials, nutrients, water, and minerals to form our body in the womb. If we didn't have that "sucking power," we could not have pulled ourselves together into physical form. If we were to suddenly lose that sucking power that holds our molecules and cells together, we couldn't exist for very long.

You can see the evidence of this primal sucking power the moment a baby is born. A newborn's very first action, if it is to live, is to suck air into its lungs. That is the moment we consider it a live birth. The second sucking action of a newborn, if it is allowed, is to suck at its mother's breast. A baby can inhale and nurse by instinct immediately because it is programmed with that sucking power.

The infant's dominant sucking power will cause it to pull anything it touches into its mouth. But it's not only its mouth that sucks; if its little fingers can grab anything at all, that sucking power will also cause its hand to instantly grip and hold very tightly. A mother knows this if they've ever had a baby grab their hair or their earring. You can't pry its grip loose!

That sucking power extends even beyond the baby's mouth and hands—beyond its own physical body. Just look at how the presence of a baby sucks in the love and attention of everyone in the room! You can't pull yourself away.

Yet this sucking power is also a burden. It is what entraps us in this physical dimension. That sucking power keeps us—our spirit and soul—stuck inside this body.

Imagine if you were locked in an automobile at birth. For your entire life, you could never get out of that car! If you wanted to eat, eliminate, sleep, interact with others, go anywhere, too bad—you would have to do it from inside of your car. Wouldn't that be a living nightmare?

This is a very accurate analogy for human life and why we suffer. That sucking power traps us inside the vehicle of a frail and limited human form. That's why Lao Tzu worries in the *Tao Te Ching*, "*The reason I have misfortune is because I have a body.*"

When we exist in physical form, we're in a double bind. We have a high level of inward, restrictive force that holds our substance together. Yet that same force that holds us together also has an expanding Yang nature that wants more freedom to move outward, to escape, to return back to the unlimited dimension it's accustomed to.

The most important thing we need to understand about this inward "sucking power" is that it is not just physical. Even beyond infancy, it permeates our very souls and forms an integral part of our human nature.

If we're honest about it, the driving force in our human life is to pull more and more into ourselves. We spend the majority of our day pulling in air, food, money, and experiences. We are programmed to want to pull more and more into ourselves for our survival. Our desires are based in seeking to pull in more love, more security, more acknowledgments, more longevity, more power, more sex, etc. The sucking power is still just as active as it was when we were a baby. The only difference is that now we know that sucking force as *greed*.

Human greed is evidence of that sucking power still at work. We cannot help ourselves. Greed is woven into our very nature and part of our survival instinct. If we had zero greed force, we would have no hunger to tell us when we need fuel, no thirst to tell us when to hydrate, no craving for companionship or sex to reproduce and raise offspring, and no drive to provide for those offspring, no reason to work.

It is critical that we understand this natural inclination toward greed if we are to understand human nature and our world. It is not necessarily a moral issue but a force deep within us. It can never be entirely eliminated as long as we walk this Earth because it's a natural consequence of the inward force that helps hold us together.

If we don't understand that greed is part of our makeup, we will never learn how to manage this burden and how to factor it into creating a balanced life for either ourselves or our society. And worse, we will not understand the second most powerful force in human life: our outward or "Yang" force.

In human life, our Yang force comes close on the heels of our Yin force. After all, what is the second thing a newborn does after it inhales and just before it is put to the breast to suck? It screams its head off! And that Yang or outward force is strong. Have you ever seen an infant vomit if it hasn't been burped? That stuff will shoot out of its mouth like a rocket!

A baby's early life is Yin and Yang as its most basic. The main issues are what is going into the baby and what is coming out of the baby.

Just like our human "sucking power" is the root of greed, our human Yang power takes on the primary force of anger.

In our lives, there will be many situations where our greed for more will not or cannot be fulfilled. As infants, the milk bottle will eventually run dry. Mother will forget to change our cold, wet diaper at least once. And nobody seems to care that we want them to pick us up from our crib no matter how hard we cry. So we scream even more!

As adults, there will also be times life does not go our way. Whatever we are grasping for will be out of reach. Our stock portfolio will crash. Our co-worker will beat us out of that promotion. The car we want will be too expensive.

When our greed is unfulfilled, we react, be it through frustration, retaliation, outrage, jealousy, vengefulness, despair, or any number of negative emotions and behaviors. These reactions are all variations of the outward force or anger, or our Yang. It's the second most powerful aspect of human nature.

That explosive force of human anger is primal and strong, just like our greed. Even Lao Tzu admits a baby can cry all day long and not get hoarse. The only way to shut it up is usually to give it something to suck.

These two Yin and Yang powers, sucking in and screaming out, greed and anger, are so strongly bound together, you cannot be human and have one without the other.

DAY DREAM, NIGHT DREAM

Examining how that bellows action of DO works can help us understand the ins and outs of birth and death.

Earlier, we looked at sub-atomic particles and how they blink in and out of our reality, appearing and then disappearing like magic. When those particles blink out of our view, they are not "gone;" it's just that we can no longer see them in our dimension. They still exist, but they exist somewhere else in another dimension, temporarily out of view.

To understand the appearing and disappearing act that particles do, consider the Sun. To us, the Sun rises and sets each day, seemingly appearing and then disappearing again, over and over. In fact, in ancient days, they believed the Sun died every night, and a new Sun was born every day.

Today, we understand that even though it seems to disappear, when the Sun rises in the morning, it is still the same Sun we saw yesterday. It's not a new Sun. The same Sun we saw yesterday never "died." The Sun only seems to disappear and reappear because of our Earth's rotation on its axis. At night, even when we can't see the Sun, we now know that it still exists. It's simply shining on the other half of the world where we can't see it.

Just like our Sun, when those particles blink and disappear, they don't cease to exist either. Like the flat-Earth believers of yesterday, our framework of knowledge is just too small to understand the whole picture of where they go. The blinking particles are merely cycling through a different dimension on their way to returning again. They go in and out of the original dimension—Dimension One.

We are like that Sun and those blinking particles too. We are born, and we die—appear and disappear. But do we completely cease to exist when we die? Not exactly. Just like those particles and the Sun, after we die, we fall out of view and exist somewhere else. Our lives are subject to that bellows like everything else; we move in and out of this dimension, back and forth.

It's true that when we die, our physical form disintegrates. But there is one part of us that cannot be destroyed, and that is the portion of DO inside of us. That piece of DO inside of us is special. Our own small piece of nothingness that holds us together is what gives us life and consciousness. We'll talk more about that later.

This piece of "nothing" has been continually within us from birth. It won't disintegrate at our death because it doesn't belong to Earth the way the minerals, water, and dust of our bodies do. It belongs to Dimension One. And this DO-infused piece of us will reappear again at another time, in another place, much like those particles winking in and out of our observation.

But when we do reappear, our little piece of DO won't magically pop up again out of nowhere as the exact same John, Barbara, or Tom we were before. That original energy that once was inside us will take a new form and appear in a new location, much like many of those particles change form and locations when they wink and blink in and out of existence.

We actually practice going in and out of our dimension every day. When? During sleep! There is some point in time during sleep when we are completely gone—completely disconnected from our body and the awareness of the human dimension around us. There is also a period during sleep when we dream.

While we acknowledge dreaming as a natural event, we don't acknowledge what goes on in dreams as real. We think our night dreams are fake and our daytime life is real. But in a way, both our dream reality and waking reality aren't as "real" as we think.

When we are awake, our thinking is more like a daydream. Why are our waking thoughts like a dream? Because we spend most of the day in our heads, absorbed in our thoughts, even though most of them mean nothing and spin on and on forever. We all have a thousand thoughts a day coming in and out of our minds on hundreds of topics. Most of them are spontaneous and out of our control, just like a dream.

Watch your undirected thoughts sometime. Do you know where they're coming from or where they go? No! See, it's just like a dream. During the day, mind activity creates random thoughts in your head, and at night mind activity creates random movie scenes for you to star in.

Sometimes the scenarios in our dreams are absolutely fantastic! We could be chased by a tiger, or fly in a spaceship, or enter a whole new world made of water and cotton candy. That's why when we wake up, we think of our dream world as unreal. It has no basis in reality, no truth.

Actually, I'm offering the view that our daytime lives are just as fake because most of what we think about all day isn't real either. It just isn't true. It's just as random and based in artificial constructs as our dream world.

If you write down everything you think about and consider real in this world, you will find that most of it isn't. The language we use—is that real? If somebody says something "good" to me, I feel very happy. If they insult me, I get very angry. But what if I don't speak German, and somebody comes up and says the same good remark to me in German or the same insult in German? It means nothing, and I don't react because language isn't real. It's just an idea we use to make communication of our thoughts to one another more convenient. When you go to South America, you speak Portuguese or Spanish, then, when you go to Sweden, you speak Swedish, and when you go to Japan, you speak Japanese. Language isn't *real*; it's an artificial construct. Most of what we consider real, like currency, names, government laws, or roles in society, are all just agreements we make on ideas, tools to get by. They aren't real beyond our own minds.

Likewise, most of our thinking is based upon these unreal concepts. Our minds take it one step further and use these unreal concepts to create unreal scenarios. When we think about the future, our imaginings, plans, wishes, and speculations, none of it is truly real. In this way, our thinking is like dreaming—just a movie playing inside our heads by our mind's constant activity.

But there are also ways day dreams and night dreams differ. In my day dream, if a tiger is coming, I can run and hide or turn and fight the tiger. During the daytime, I have the option of action. As an awake human being, I can move around in this dimension.

During the night time, however, you are in a different dimension where your consciousness and thinking are disconnected from your body. Your motion and what you do next aren't always up to you. While you can watch yourself "do" many things in a dream, they don't affect this human dimension where your body is sleeping. And in the dream, you can't affect your dream body either. You are mostly at the mercy of your mind in how you move, think or what happens to you in your dream.

When you think about it, being in a dimension where you don't control your body, and can't run away from a tiger sounds terrible, right? It normally would make you feel powerless and out of control with no ability to consciously act on your own behalf. Everything is pre-scripted for you by your mind. And yet, most people hate to wake up from a dream. We want the experience to go on and on and never get up. We love it and want to return rather than get up and face this waking life when our alarm goes off most mornings. "Just a few more minutes please!"

Likewise, our waking life is dominated by our thoughts which are based in false ideas. No matter how hollow they are, we follow our thoughts and ideas like a script. Just like in a dream, we often feel out of control in our lives, and are forced to deal with random tragedies, or are elated by windfall moments of joy and pleasure. It's not that much different than trying to run away from tigers in our night dreams. We just have a bit more control and conscious direction in how we react mentally and physically to the events in our waking world than we do in a dream. But that's also a lot of work.

And just like waking from a dream – at the end of our lives, we don't want to leave. The alarm says our time is up in our daydream world, but we want so badly to stay and experience it some more. "Just a few more minutes please!"

Our constant back and forth between our day dream and night dream is another form of that bellows in motion. We move in and out, back and forth. We have little choice in the matter as nature demands that we sleep at some point. After we sleep, at some point, we wake up. And after we've been awake all day, at some point we sleep. And when we can't sleep and wake normally, it feels like suffering to us. A constant cycle of sleeping and waking is part of what keeps us alive—it's an inescapable part of our human nature.

Our alternating day dreams and night dreams function like an energy wave: First, it's daytime, and you are in your day dream and moving around here in the waking world; then, at night time, your mind activity carries on as you drop down into your night dream.

Day dream, night dream, day dream, night dream, day dream, night dream—it is the inward and outward, up and down, bellows action on our consciousness. But through it all, your ability to think stays intact. Your belief that you are still the same person each morning, living the same continuous life as yesterday's day dream, is also still intact.

Day Dream

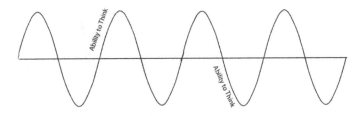

Night Dream

Part Two: The Bellows

If you have a sweet dream, that's good—it's as if you are in paradise or in heaven. And if you have a nightmare, it's as if you are in hell. During those nightmares you *want* to wake up, and are so relieved when you do.

We count on the fact that every morning, like a miracle, we come back from unconsciousness and the dream state to the waking human world. This can happen when people are in a coma too. They slip away to somewhere else but then miraculously come back.

If you are sleeping or in a coma, we don't call you dead. We know that there is a probability that you will come back and your mind and your ability to think will be intact, and you will be the same as before—as long as you haven't suffered any physical damage to your brain.

We count on the fact – whether in a coma, under anesthesia, or in a deep, restful sleep – that the real "us" hasn't disappeared, but will resurface into the waking world with our awareness fully functional again. These are like our practice runs at disappearing into another dimension and returning again! We soon relax into the fact that we can pop up and down, in and out of the waking human world and be okay.

We put our trust in this process every night—that our human mind and awareness can shut down and go to another dimension and still return.

In this life, we experience a lot of "daytime." In fact, it's this string of daytimes that we label as our "life." It's what matters, what counts to us as living. But, in a way, that's not really true. Our daytime life is more like a flicker. The truth is we sleep and wake, sleep and wake, day dream, night dream, day dream, night dream, live, die, live, die, live, die. But because of our many daytimes, we consider ourselves to be continuously alive. Those broken pieces we call days form what feels like a continuous stream. It's like that projector's light shining through a rapid sequence of thousands of still picture frames that allow us to watch a movie. Our daytimes strung together form the movie of our lives.

But one day, this up and down of daydreams and night dreams becomes disorganized. As people sicken or age, their sleeping and waking become erratic and unpredictable. At the same time, their thinking becomes confused. One day, they slip out of their body and never come back. When that happens, we say Grandma is "dead." We go ahead and bury her because we know that her ability to think is no longer coming back to assume her body.

But that doesn't mean that Grandma is gone forever. That part of Grandma that formed her ability to think keeps going in another dimension without her body.

Before the day your body expires, you will have exercised that in-your-body, out-of-your-body, in-your-body, out-of-your body, in and out, thousands of times. When we reach the end of our lives, that continuous awareness that lies in our pure ability to think doesn't disappear. You've just relocated to the other side of that bellows. That part of you that forms your "ability to think" carries on in another dimension.

What we knew as "Grandma" may even return to human life or Earth in a different lifetime or form, just like those particles that disappear and appear again or our Sun that seems to die each evening as it vanishes from sight, only to rise again in the morning.

Our body belongs to Earth, so it will deteriorate and die. Our mind is different. It's made of eternal, indestructible DO. That's why, as people age, they still think like when they were young. Their mind keeps going. Unless you have damage to the physical hardware of your brain, the part that belongs to Earth, your ability to think doesn't age. That's why your awareness, your sense of consciousness, never feels like it gets any older.

If you ask most older people if their mind feels any different than 20 years ago (other than maybe feeling forgetful—a hardware problem in the brain), most people say, "No." An eighty-year-old still feels her conscious self to be just as alive and the same as she did when she was 40 or 30 or 20.

The root of your ability to think belongs to DO. It doesn't age because it isn't subject to the laws of space or time. As such, it isn't susceptible to the laws of Earth, age, and decay. It's your very own piece of that fabric of the universe.

While your piece of DO isn't subject to Earth's laws, it *is* subject to the laws of DO. If we don't know those laws, we lose out on making the most of our lives. When we learn how the laws of DO apply to us and to our ability to think, our potential in life expands infinitely.

PART THREE

THE ONE POWER

*"These things since ancient times all arise from
the ultimate One Power:
Heaven is formed by the ultimate One Power and is clear,
The Earth is also formed by the ultimate One Power
and is stable,
The gods are all powered by the ultimate One Power
and become spiritually functional,
The rivers receive the only One Power and become full.
The ten thousand things, created by the only One Power,
through it become alive."*

Tao Te Ching, Chapter 39

STILLNESS AND MOTION

In our sub-particle world, nothing and something are forever interchanging. That being the case, how does nothingness turn into something? Let's turn to another analogy for DO that Lao Tzu used all the time: water.

Imagine DO as water in a vast lake. If you look at a large stretch of water that is perfectly calm, its glass-like surface can make it look as if nothing is there. It is perfectly reflective, perfectly clear, perfectly still. But if a wind or current crosses that water, you will see ripples and know, "Aha! Water is there!" It's the waves that make the water's surface visible. This is how a lake in perfect stillness can look completely different from a lake in motion. Yet whether its surface is still and clear or wavy and visible, both are the same lake, the same water.

Just like that lake, the nothingness of Dimension One can be either in a state of stillness or in a state of motion. When DO is in its original stillness, it is not visible, not describable in any way. It's nothing. But once it sets itself into motion, other dimensions arise and become visible. What was once nothing suddenly becomes something.

It only takes one pebble dropped on the glass-like surface of a lake to create ripples circling out from the center in all directions. If more pebbles drop here and there, the surface of the water is soon a crisscrossed network of waves, bombarding other waves. Instead of glassy nothingness, we have a patchwork of patterns, shapes, activity.

Similarly, when nothingness begins to move inward and outward, activating its Yin and Yang power, it forms ripples and waves of its very self—just like water does. That convoluted rippling of waves in the original stillness, the original nothingness, is the primal origin of all phenomena like time, space, energy, and matter. Everything we can see, hear, taste, touch, and experience is made possible by that network of rippling waves in the nothingness of DO.

NENG AND KONG

According to the ancient Taoists, Dimension One has two aspects: *Neng* and *Kong*.

Neng is the first aspect of DO. Neng is when that state of nothingness begins to think, move, and stir. Neng is DO activating its potential for action. It's the gathering force of the ocean when a wave or tide is just about to swell. Neng is the word to describe DO initiating its potential to be anything, know anything, create anything, and annihilate anything. *Neng is Dimension One moving toward action.*

Kong is the second aspect of DO. Kong is when that action and creation quiets down and begins to retreat back toward stillness. It's the wave calming down and becoming absorbed again into the calm, still, depths of the lake. *Kong* is the word to describe DO moving toward a return to perfect stillness. *Kong is Dimension One moving toward non-action.*

While Neng and Kong are another form of DO's bellows, they contain a more complex picture of its inward and outward powers.

Neng and Kong are terms we use in Taoist teaching. Similar terms are also found in western mysticism and alchemy. They use the terms "coagula" and "solve"—congeal and dissolve. Old magicians were said to be able to use these two forces to change lead into gold and that they were the root of all magic.

A Taoist would say there is nothing magical about it. Magic and miracles are just events we can't understand *yet*. To a primitive tribe in the Pacific Ocean, an airplane is a miracle, and those who fly in them are gods. To us, we understand that the pilot in the plane is made possible by scientific laws more advanced than the islanders have learned about yet.

Neng and Kong are forces inherent in DO, and everything we know is shaped by them. But they aren't magic. They are aspects of the first dimension that govern the cycle of creation, existence, change, and the return to non-existence. Like all the laws of DO, the more you know about them, the more you can cooperate with them instead of fighting against them.

NENG THINKS AND CREATES REALITY

Let's explore the properties of Neng first—the properties of DO moving toward action.

In the emptiness of DO lies the potential ability to think and create. DO's potential ability is always ready to emerge from nothingness and launch into action. We call it potential because until DO activates Neng, it hasn't quite started to think yet—because if it did, it would instantaneously create something. At this state, it just has that *potential*, that *ability*.

Neng is like a current of power within nothing that carries this immense creative potential for nothing to become something. Neng is nothingness ripe with the prospect of creating, ready to burst into the product of its own intelligence.

It is very easy to mistake DO's Neng quality as a substance. It's not a substance, but it has the potential to become a substance. It's both a temporary and a permanent state of *in-between*. DO is a condition of continual suspension between two very different states—something and nothing. Neng is the force that can tilt DO toward becoming something.

Neng is found in that in-between state—between stillness and motion. It is everywhere that DO is. It doesn't travel, nor does it have a location. It has no beginning and no end. How wide is nothingness? That is how big Neng is.

Go find a sheet of paper and set it down in front of you. That piece of paper is DO, the whole fabric of nothingness in the universe.

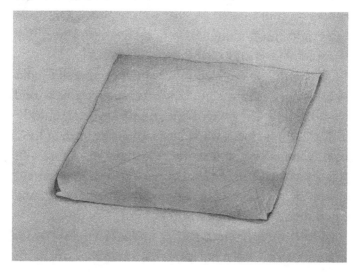

If you crinkle up that paper, that's like Neng crinkling up nothingness and space, activating its potential to create "something."

Neng is DO in action. Neng is what can crinkle up the nothingness so tightly that this crinkling creates and condenses into matter, like particles or rocks. Or, Neng can crinkle up nothingness very loosely into something less solid, like energy or thought.

Neng that is crinkled loosely, like energy, still looks like nothing—it's invisible, flows freely even through solid material, and can revert back to nothing very quickly. This is what happens when Neng takes the form of heat, light, gamma rays, and sound. We know that those substances still have a great deal of free-flowing Neng potential in them because they are invisible, penetrating, and can disperse quickly back into nothing.

Other times, Neng wrinkles up DO so tightly that it becomes solid—forming particles, molecules, rocks, or our material bodies. Neng is still in those material forms, but it's locked inside of itself as it tightly holds the matter into physical form. It has a harder time to flow, penetrate, or return back to DO.

Neng can compress space to become very dense or cause space to open up—it can wrinkle space together or unwrinkle it. Neng has infinite ability. It can create or annihilate anything; it can make that space it condensed into this book revert back into nothingness.

While it is creating, thinking, and in motion, Neng is higher and faster than any other frequency or wavelength of energy. It is ultra-invisible but also ultra-powerful. As Neng starts shrinking itself and space together, the more it shrinks, the more its frequency slows. It starts coming down to light and heat and finally, to become matter.

Matter has a lot of Neng trapped inside, and because of that, it also has a lot of energy potential locked inside as well. If Neng decides it wants to be free, those atoms will open up and allow that matter's light, electricity, radiation, and heat to all dissipate outward into nothingness, to return to DO. It is the reason that matter decays: it does so, so that Neng can escape and return to DO.

Scientists stumbled onto this tremendous pent-up force of Neng when they discovered nuclear fission and nuclear fusion. That explosive release of Neng as it rushes out and back into nothing is immensely powerful.

The couch I'm sitting on is made of space. So is the pen I'm writing with. Neng is space itself as well as the force that can pull space together. Neng is crinkling up space very tightly to become the wood and upholstery of my couch, pen, and even you as you read this.

Neng pulls in the emptiness to create the matter, thoughts, and living energy of everything that surrounds us. We and our world are made of and part of Dimension One through the fabric of Neng. But, we have a hard time seeing or believing there is such a fabric, as we are very distracted by the outer events and experiences of the life we lead.

Here's an analogy to understand the fabric of Neng relative to our lives: When we watch a movie in a theater, what are we really staring at? Art? A story? Moving pictures? Flashing colors made possible by the light of a projector? Yes, to all. Yet, there is something we don't see that makes the movie possible: a screen.

A movie screen is just a big piece of cloth stretched across a frame. But we forget about that fabric because we're totally distracted by the pictures and the story projected onto it.

One time in a small town, a bunch of kids crept into the back door of a movie theater so they could watch a movie for free. The owner found out and kicked them out on the street, telling them never to come back.

The next week, those kids got back at that cranky movie theater owner. They decided to sneak in again, but this time they brought a pigeon with them and a bottle of ink. Once the bright flickering lights of the film began, they dipped the pigeon's feet in ink and let it go. The pigeon, attracted by the light of the movie and thinking it was the open outdoor sky, flew right into the screen, leaving big black streaks of ink on it. The screen was now ruined because when people came to watch the movie, they would now notice the screen. Noticing the screen meant they couldn't just forget about it and enjoy the movie.

This book is a little like that pigeon, throwing ink on the fabric of DO so we can remember that it's there. But it's important to learn about the screen—the Neng pulling in and weaving the fabric of existence out of nothingness that makes the movie of our lives possible.

Neng is only the first aspect of the power and potential within DO—remember, there is also Kong.

KONG STRUGGLES TO RETURN TO NOTHING

Whenever Neng crinkles up nothing into the forms of energy or matter, it always carries with it the Kong nature of DO. They are inseparable, just like Yin and Yang. Kong, by its nature, is always trying to return to the original state of DO in stillness. Kong is that force of DO returning to non-action.

Kong is why energy in any form will dissipate sooner or later and why we have entropy. Entropy is energy moving from a state of usefulness (form) toward chaos or an unusable state (no form). Those energy particles like electrons are pulled together by Neng. But because they also have Kong, the force inside them also desperately wants to escape and return to DO. Lao Tzu talks about the nature of Kong in chapter 41 of the *Tao Te Ching* when he says: *"The Tao moves in the direction of returning."*

Neng and Kong work opposite each other. Neng is working to hold things together in creation, to move, to be, to exist, while Kong is working to escape, to return, and to rest again. This eternal dual is why everything is in a constant state of change. This is why things arise and fall, are created and destroyed, amplify, then dissipate. It is an interchange that goes on constantly and simultaneously, forever.

Because of Kong, all matter will decay over time. Decay and decomposition are the Kong within matter trying desperately to return and revert back into its natural state of nothingness and stillness in DO. As Neng begins to relax in response to Kong, the force holding the matter together degrades.

Scientists can use sensitive photon equipment to show that everything emits some measure of light—rocks, plants, all living and even non-living things. That light is energy trying to escape back into space. It's visual evidence of decay as electrons escape. They are also viewing the force of Kong in action, trying to return.

That's what decay is: a determination to return. Neng pulls the nothingness of DO together where it is trapped inside of things called heat, electrons, neutrons, magnetic force, a stone, a plant. It doesn't matter how dense or tough a substance is; if you give it enough time, the other side of DO's nature, Kong, will begin to decay and destroy the object and try to escape back into space. Eventually, after days, years, eons, it will become space again. If we could view it from the lens of DO, the speed and beauty of that process are dazzling.

This is why nothing lasts forever, except for DO. Everything deteriorates, dissipates, falls apart, changes, and disappears over time. It is the force inside of everything struggling to return to DO. Eventually, Kong will succeed. Everything will return to the nothingness of DO once again. Yet, once there, what returns will also be re-engaged again by Neng and summoned forth back into a new creation, new movement, new form of DO in action.

Everything we know moves from creation to return and return to creation; from rest to activity, and activity to rest. That's why everything is more or less just a wave appearing on that lake of DO. Some waves are bigger, some waves are smaller, and some travel across a wide ocean for a long time. Some calm down and return back to stillness more quickly than others.

As human beings, we have that Neng force. Neng is what created our bodies and is holding us together. Our Neng pulls in the minerals, water, food, and material necessary to sustain our physical being. The high energy of Neng in our bodies is what gives us life and the ability to think. But the Kong force inside of us also continually seeks to escape and return to DO. So ultimately, our bodies change, age, die, and decay, thanks to the force of Kong.

Dimension One always contains both Neng and Kong potential. Moreover, these two abilities—the ability to move and the ability not to move—cannot be separated. They are both inherent abilities contained in nothingness and cannot be peeled apart. So you will never find Neng without Kong, and you will never find Kong without Neng.

There is a conundrum here, however. Once Neng begins to move and creation starts, DO is disturbed, and waves form to pull space and nothingness together to become "something." At that point, it is no longer pure Dimension One anymore. Creation has begun. It is now automatically Dimension Two and may rapidly evolve into additional dimensions as the activity of that thinking, movement, and action ripple outward. But underneath, in the underlying emptiness, the active potential of Neng and the returning potential of Kong are always there. They exist everywhere, in everything, as part of the ever-present nothingness. They are another footprint of DO.

DO IS THE ABILITY TO THINK!

If a bike is parked in front of us, we can easily push or squeeze the surface of the bicycle tire to check if it needs air. The tire is easy to press down when it's standing still. However, don't try to check the air pressure in a bicycle tire while it's still moving! That same tire is much harder to push down if it's spinning. When it spins, the surface of a bicycle tire becomes firm and harder to grasp.

An atom is a lot like that bicycle tire but even more amazing. Instead of a solid rubber tire spinning, an atom is surrounded with what is more like two or three small particles of rubber spinning fast enough to produce the appearance and function of a whole tire. An atom's electrons, neutrons, and protons are spinning around each other so fast that we can neither squeeze them nor see through them to detect how much nothingness is inside that atom.

An atom seems like a sphere, but an atom can be just one neutron and one electron. The reason it takes up space and projects the surface and volume of a sphere is because that one electron moves around so quickly. The electron not only moves around but in, out, and through the neutron. When I hypothetically look at or touch that atom, I think it is a solid ball because that electron moves so fast.

Part Three: The One Power

Yet if we could stop the spinning and look even closer, we'd realize that the neutron and electron are both empty. We'd see the underlying truth about matter is that solidity is produced by empty spinning around empty to make "hard."

But let's take this observation one step further: We can agree then that what makes matter solid isn't the particles at all. What makes matter solid is its "ability to spin."

What makes that electron spin? Can you draw that? No, because it's empty. The forces that make those particles spin around each other are positive and negative charges—pulling or pushing, attracting or repulsing. Again, these forces are just another manifestation of inward and outward, Yin and Yang—the two primal forces of DO. They're invisible and without substance. They're nothing. But we know they're there by the way they work.

The "ability to spin" is a small illustration, a small fragment of a much greater universal truth of DO. *DO also carries the most powerful ability of all—the "ability to think."*

Yes. That's correct! Another ultimate truth about nothingness that permeates everything and creates everything we know is that it has the ability to think. "Nothing" has intelligence!

Nobody created the "ability to think." It's always been there, inherent in the Neng quality of nothingness.

You may be asking, "How can non-living physical matter and energy, not to mention nothingness, have the ability to think?"

When we consider all the different forms of energy, matter, and beings in our universe, the range of this ability and potential to think is a very wide range indeed. This includes the lower ranges of thinking that we find in what we currently consider inanimate objects, like particles or energy, all the way up to the higher, more sophisticated ranges of thinking, such as our own human ability to think.

When we look at that electron whirling within an atom, we can observe how particles in matter "think." Particles aren't stupid; they just think in very limited and stubborn ways like "hug right, hug right, hug right" or "orbit, orbit, orbit." An electron has the "intelligence" to seek balance with a proton.

A particle can only think in this very short range until it decays. When it decays, that Kong power takes over and returns all the Neng potential originally held within that atom to the nothingness and stillness of DO. When that happens, the atom deteriorates, and its ability to think returns to stillness and rest.

The most important effect of the first dimension on our lives is that it gives us the ability to think. *We* can think because *DO* can think. The root of our power to think comes from the emptiness inside of us. Inside that emptiness is the Neng that is thinking, creating, and holding us together. And since Neng has that ability to think, and Neng makes up our entire being, we in turn also have the ability to think.

Neng's ability to think is dispersed throughout our body and functions in many ways. Consider your cells. The cells in your liver are performing dozens of life-sustaining functions for you every minute that you, thankfully, never have to consciously think about. Those cells already know everything they need to know to do the job. They have their own "intelligence." How do they have that with no schooling, no conscious direction from your mind? They have intelligence because they are made from Neng.

Remember, too, that Neng is the "ability" to think. It doesn't mean that the emptiness is always thinking. It just has that ability. You have the ability to think, but you aren't necessarily always thinking. Sometimes, you go into a deep enough sleep where your thinking shuts off for a while, or perhaps you are knocked unconscious. You aren't thinking during those times, but you still have the ability to think.

Famous philosopher René Descartes observed: "I think, therefore I am." The trouble with humans is that we confuse our thoughts and thinking with our *ability to think*. They are two different things entirely. While the ability to think is an ultimate truth we inherit from DO, our thinking itself, those thoughts that come and go, are just byproducts of that.

We think that our collection of thoughts, memories, and feelings are who we are. But are our thoughts really us? Are they the truest part of us? How can they be if they are changing all the time? Try to count all the many different thoughts you think in just one day and all the different moods they spark. If your thinking is you, that means you have thousands of different selves every day!

Our thinking changes every second, but what never changes is that ability to think, the nature of it. That's why the ultimate truth of us and who we are is far more constant than our passing-thought life. That constancy lies just underneath our thoughts: It is our ability to think. It's our ability to think that defines us as conscious and fully alive. Our ability to think is the constant that remains the same throughout our stages of life, at every age, despite any mood, event, or current train of thought.

And it's precisely because we are so wrapped up in *what* we think that we hardly ever notice our *ability* to think. We are too busy using it to give it the consideration it deserves.

There is an old Chinese tale of a foolish cow herder. He wasn't very bright, so herding cows was the only job he could manage to do. His uncle hired him and showed him how to count his ten cows so that when it was time to take them home from the pasture, the nephew could count them and know that they were all there before putting them safely back in the barn.

Day after day, the cowherd brought his uncle's cows to pasture, and then at day's end, he counted each of them on his fingers: 1-2-3-4-5-6-7-8-9-10, before he herded them back into the barn.

One day, there was a blistering heatwave. The poor cow herder was hot and exhausted from being out in the pasture all day. He shuffled slowly on his way home with his cows. A passerby shouted at him: "Hey stupid! Why not just ride one of those cows and make your trip home easier?"

The cow herder thought this was a smart idea. It would be less effort for him than walking in the hot sun! So, he climbed on the back of one of the cows and rode happily all the way back to his uncle's farm.

When he got to the barn, he counted his cows: 1-2-3-4-5-6-7-8-9. "Oh no!" said the cowherd. "I only have nine cows! I lost one!"

He panicked. He knew his uncle, who owned the cows, would be very upset. He counted them again, and still, there were only nine. He was fretting and counting them over and over but always counted only nine.

Finally, his uncle came out from the farmhouse to see why his nephew had not yet put the cows in the barn. "Oh, Uncle," the cowherd cried. "Please don't beat me. I have lost one of your cows. I counted them so many times, but I only have nine."

Now the uncle was very smart and looked at the situation carefully. He said, "Nephew, I think I know what is wrong. Have you ever ridden one of the cows home before?"

"No, uncle, I only thought of it today when someone yelled at me on the road and told me to. It seemed like a good idea since it was such a hot day."

"Okay, nephew, get down off the cow and count them again."

So the dim-witted cowherd climbed off the back of the cow he was riding and counted his cows again. Miraculously, there were ten cows once more.

That tenth cow is like our ability to think that we continually ride on. It's the cow we miss.

You have that ability, I have that ability, everyone has that ability to think. And although your thoughts and my thoughts on any given day are probably very different, there is a great similarity between the mechanism—the root ability—of how you think and how I think.

Most people have similar basic thinking functions and patterns, or we could never have the sciences of psychiatry, neurology, psychology, sociology, or behavioral studies. The overall sameness between human beings and the patterns of how we think point to the fact that our thinking ability comes from a common source, the same root. So, while what you and I think may be different, our ability to think comes from the same DO.

Now human beings are more intelligent than a rock or a tree; so our thinking is more complicated and of a higher level. Some people also have more intelligence than others. But whether it is the simple intelligence of the quark that blinks in and out at just the right time, or the "thinking" of a flower when it turns toward the Sun, or the dog's ecstatic tail wagging when it sees its owner coming up the sidewalk, or the intellect of the liver's cells as they filter out toxins from the blood—the root source of these functions are no different. In each case, the ability to think comes from the same source, the Neng force of DO.

The secret the Taoists discovered is that when they dove underneath their thoughts and thinking and firmly connected only to their *ability to think,* they were suddenly able to access the all-knowing potential of DO—a knowing that transcends time and space, that penetrates all barriers and limitations. That ability to think became like a superhighway of information to them that they could ride at will.

That ability to think is connected to Neng, which is part of the nothingness that is one piece and extends and connects everything, everywhere. When one touches the ability to think, the potential of that ability is unlimited.

The difference between our thoughts and our ability to think is a subtle one to feel and connect to inside. It takes practice, sincerity, and methods preserved by generations of Taoist masters to accomplish, but it's a real connection that many successfully made.

When we start out on a path of meditation or Tao practice, we don't believe we can tap into that ability because we are blocked by our own limited thinking. It's as if we have our hands covering our eyes and are crying, "I can't see, I can't see!" But if you take away your hands, you find that you always had the ability to see. Your biggest challenge is to move your own thinking aside, like taking the hands away from your eyes.

EVOLUTION OR DEVOLUTION

The ultimate truth of DO is that everything springs forth from the potential within nothingness through the action of Neng. As Neng pulls in nothingness tighter and tighter into form, those forms become progressively denser. The least dense forms are the many variations of energy. Then, there are the many types of life forms in the middle ranges, and finally, there are different types of solid matter.

Less dense are things like light, heat, X-rays, and gamma rays. Denser items are gasses, liquids, and atomic elements. Even more dense are molecules that make up physical matter. The more loosely a form is bound, the higher, faster, and subtler things are, and the closer they are to DO. The more tightly bound a form is, the slower, more substantial, heavy, and solid they are, the further they are from DO.

This challenges the man-made concept of evolution. Evolution theory proposes that particles in the form of primordial mud were charged with energy to become the building blocks of life. From such charged particles, the theory claims, simple life forms evolved, such as the virus, amoeba, and then the earthworm. That earthworm evolved over many eons and mutations into a monkey, then that monkey evolved into primitive ancestors of homo sapiens on up to the more sophisticated human beings we are today.

According to the theory of evolution, the heavy, dense, slow mud is the root, and the invisible energies of life and thought are the branches that grow from it over time. If the theory of evolution were true, that would mean that our ability to think grew from a rock.

Our modern culture is deeply programmed to think that we are still evolving up and out of the mud. We believe we are continually getting smarter and better. Since we cannot envision what sort of creature-body we will evolve into in order to hold this imagined self-growth, we work on computers and robotics to house our minds once our bodies die so that we can keep evolving ever upward.

Others embrace the evolution theory in spiritual or religious terms. They think that we will transmute ourselves into spiritual beings and even evolve to an otherworldly state closer to that of a god. This "ascension" or "evolution programming" colors many religious and spiritual paths. The root of the belief, however, is that we are still climbing further and further out of the mud.

What we are really claiming when we embrace a theory of evolution, and especially when we follow it with a religious or spiritual belief in human ascension and all its ramifications, is that a particle can eventually become God.

What the truth of DO proclaims is the *opposite* of evolution: That consciousness and the ability to think began with nothing and ended with a particle. If we want to have more power and potential, we must not keep dragging our mud into brave new worlds but instead go backward and find our original source, that potent "nothingness" from which we are created, and that holds the power of consciousness within.

The *Tao Te Ching*, the *Bible*, and many Buddhist Sutras offer support for this reverse theory that tips evolution on its head. Their scriptures all ultimately say the same thing about the origin of the universe: In the beginning, there is nothingness or a void or an abyss, but this nothingness has the ability to think.

This ultimate thinking is not like our ordinary thinking or comprehension. Whatever this original ability thinks, it instantly creates! It can generate something from nothing. This ability has no beginning and no end, knows everything, and is everywhere at the same time.

When we move further away from that original source, that pure creating mind of DO, we don't evolve, we devolve! Once anything is created from and by that first dimension of nothingness, that creation has already stepped down from the fullness of that original power. It now no longer possesses the infinite potential of the original DO. As a "creation," it becomes less somehow in that it is now defined and set apart as "not-DO," constricted as opposed to the free-flowing nothingness it came from.

DO initiates creation from the subtle downward, from nothingness into energy and *only then* into solid matter—in that order. The closer a creation is to the nature and ability of DO, the more free-flowing, powerful, intelligent, invisible, and subtle it is. Its resemblance is closer to "nothing."

The bad news is that if you find yourself as a physical being in the physical world, focusing only on what is material and visible around you, looking to the physical world and physical sciences for answers, you are not evolving. In fact, you are retarding and devolving from the full capability and nature of that origin. You are worshiping a particle religion and facing a direction of devolution, not evolution. You are building castles in the mud.

THE UNCARVED BLOCK

When we say we come from mud and are ascending to God, we adopt a view that we are separate beings working to rejoin the whole. In fact, our predicament is caused by doing exactly the opposite: We've always been part of the whole, but we've worked very hard to separate ourselves from it and see ourselves as individual beings. We keep devolving as we strengthen our sense of self-hood, our ego, our "I." Our separation is our own making and lies in the artificial way we think.

We can never separate ourselves from DO. We are made of it and thus carry it around inside of us and are surrounded by it every second, every breath, with every thought and action. But nonetheless we try to separate ourselves all the time. Not only do we try and separate ourselves as "I" or "Jane" or "Sam," but we try and separate everything around us from DO too.

Humans have a separation bias. It's more convenient for us if we see each person in the world as a distinct individual. It's also more convenient for us if we see thoughts, actions, events, objects, animals, and everything in our environment as separate and distinct. We give everything its own "name," we set boundaries around everything (like parentheses separating a complete sentence). We

Part Three: The One Power

never consider that everything is connected and part of one piece, one totality.

My desktop is covered with a big paper calendar that I can doodle on or write down important appointments. I can see the whole month of January at one glance. My calendar offers a great analogy for how we think versus what is the truth.

JANUARY 2022

SUN	MON	TUE	WED	THU	FRI	SAT
						1
2	3	4	5	6	7	8
9	10	11	12	13	14	15
16	17	18	19	20	21	22
23	24	25	26	27	28	29
30	31					

Because I have a name, I think I'm separate. I'm like January 15th on the calendar. I feel special. I have my own little box, and there is no other number exactly like me. I can see there are lots of other numbers around me. We all are different and have our own boxes. But we are all "January," so we feel we are very important.

Now some of the numbers feel even *more* important. January 1st likes to strut around a lot and tell everyone it's very special because it's something called "New Year's

Day." The other numbers argue back that the 1st is just the same as any other box.

There are some numbers that think they're more important too, like arrogant 29, 30, or 31 – very special indeed. The higher numbers all have their own little fancy neighborhood down at the bottom of the page. The rest of us aren't allowed to go there; we're not high enough. Nobody knows what happens outside of the calendar—we hear there are other worlds like September, July, and April.

We are as silly as the numbers on my calendar. Why? Because while we argue and consider our world, we forgot the most important thing of all: the paper. We are all just printed marks on that same white sheet of paper and are nothing without it. Any illusion that we are somehow separate from it and each other is only a superficial appearance.

January 15th can't get up and walk away from the calendar, and neither can January 1st because they are just a part of that same paper—no different, really. Any concept of separation or qualitative difference between one date from another is all an idea in our minds.

In the same way, if I isolate a piece of this ancient origin, DO, and say: "I think; therefore I am," I just cut myself off from my oneness with the origin. I've claimed a little piece of this infinity as "me" and "mine." I forgot about the paper.

"...the original Te within becomes resourceful, and it becomes the state of the original uncarved block.
The original uncarved material can be made into countless useful products."

Tao Te Ching, Chapter 28

Everything produced, everything named, is actually still part of that uncarved block. Though we think we can carve ourselves off of it, we can never separate from it. We simply prefer the idea that things are separate because it's more convenient for us. It helps us run our lives and think about reality in more efficient ways.

Yet it's all the same uncarved block. Time is one piece, space is one piece, and energy is one piece. If you say "today," today is no more than me pinching a piece of this fabric together and labeling it "today." Even if I separate it in my head as something distinct, today isn't separate from time. Time remains one piece, no matter how I think about it or label it.

This is true even of many of the physical objects in our lives. We are connected to so much around us in ways we are oblivious to.

For example, we generally ignore the Sun, even though it's always there, sustains our life, and is an integral part of everything we see and do. We feel we can ignore the Sun because we like to think of ourselves as separate from the Sun. But are we?

Where is the boundary of the Sun? At the limit of its physical mass? Beyond its mass, the Sun's radiation and energy are shining out in all directions very far. If you looked at our Sun from another star, you would not even see our planet; it would be absorbed in the sphere of light that is our Sun. We are right in it, continually immersed in its energy field of light, heat, and radiation. We are part of it and its domain. We are not as separate from the Sun as we'd like to think. Everything touched by its heat, radiation, and light are connected in some way to the Sun.

This is just like DO. The one-piece fabric of ultimate origin has no limitations or boundaries. We are always in it and never separate. The only thing that gives us the illusion that we are separate is our lack of awareness of this fact.

Just because clouds cover the Sun and we cannot see it doesn't mean it is not there. Clouds just block our awareness of the Sun and give a greater illusion that we are separate from it. They may even block our ability to feel the Sun's warmth or see its light. But the truth is that even behind those clouds, we are still the beneficiary of the Sun's heat and warmth and still immersed in its extended body of energy.

In our minds, we carry around a lot of nonsense thinking that functions much like those clouds. We are so focused on the clouds of our individual thoughts that we lose sight of the "ability to think" that connects us to and is fueled by our oneness with DO.

The biggest concept that separates us from DO is the word "I." What we consider as our "self"—a separate entity with agency and thought—is somewhat of an illusion.

Did you know that you have up to 10 pounds of bacteria in your body? That bacteria forms a large part of your immune system, helps digest your food, can create cravings and aversions to certain food, and can even affect your mood and mental health. If it can affect how you feel, what you desire, and how you think, is that bacteria "you" or separate from you?

Is the air you breathe you? When you inhale and exhale, that air mixes with your bloodstream in an intimate connection that sustains your life. If you separate yourself from the air, you will die in minutes. Therefore, we could make a case that air is an integral part of what makes "you" you.

By far, what we claim most as "I" is our thinking. We, like Descartes, consider our thoughts as "us." They define our personality, trigger our emotions, create our agenda for the day and interpret everything around us. But what allows us to think? Where and what is that consciousness, that mechanism that creates and makes thoughts possible?

That one DO—the nothingness penetrating all things and never cut off from its own wholeness—is the source of our ability to think. And that belongs to the uncarved block.

Indeed, this is unexplored territory in human knowledge. The ability to think is such a wonderful, mysterious state of our being that it's rarely noticed or understood by man.

Our mind, after babyhood, remains at a stepped-down version of the whole capability of DO precisely and ironically because we use our mind to think, blurring and covering up that true ability or true mind. So we end up with knowledge but not truth. That's why thinking must be managed and set aside, for no matter how brief a time, to allow the piece of DO that is our true mind to fully appear and shine through the clouds so it can work for us.

PART FOUR

THE NET

*"Heaven's net is ever large and wide.
Though its meshes are coarse, yet nothing slips through"*

Tao Te Ching, Chapter 73

ACTION, REACTION, AND HEAVEN'S NET

"Every action has an equal and opposite reaction," says Sir Isaac Newton's third law of motion. This action/reaction principle is the unchanging backbone of what we know and understand about physical science and the universe.

The reason this action/reaction principle *is* so immutable is that *it is a primary law of DO*, not just physics.

Every action produces an equal and opposite reaction due to the natural result of the inward and outward power of DO. How does this work?

Imagine a soccer player in training camp. He stands in front of a wide and stiff vertical rebounding net. He kicks the ball only to have it bounce back so he can kick it again. This happens over and over. Through this practice, he learns how to both kick and receive the ball.

The net makes this possible by its inward then outward reaction—the net bows inward to receive the ball from the player and then snaps back outward to transmit the ball back to the player.

We already know that Sir Newton's law of physics applies to objects and energy in the material world. But since it is also a *universal law* in Dimension One, the DO soccer net applies not only to physical matter but to everything that's intangible too. That means in DO, Sir Newton's law of physics works on invisible and subtle things like human thoughts and human actions.

Like that net, DO rebounds absolutely everything! If you send out anger, anger comes back to you. If you give someone comfort, you'll receive comfort. If you hurt someone, you will be hurt. If you steal, you will be stolen from. If you give away money, you'll receive money.

The religious observe this law in human affairs and call it karma, proclaiming "what you reap you shall sow," "as you judge, so also shall you be judged," or "do unto others what you would have them do unto you." Others simply quip, "whatever goes around comes around."

What's really happening is that DO is functioning exactly like that soccer rebounding net. Whatever you throw at it, it will return back to you—whether it be a rock, a sound wave, or a bad thought, good deed, or hurtful action.

How can DO rebound to us the qualities of our own thoughts and actions?

DO is not only the fundamental fabric underlying energy and matter but also the fundamental fabric underlying mind, thoughts, and life energy. That's what makes it an ultimate truth—it applies to everything! This means that all the universal laws of DO apply to both tangible *and intangible* phenomena.

When DO is in stillness like that smooth and perfectly calm lake, nothing is acting or reacting. But the minute DO starts to move, the action/reaction principle is immediately switched on. That first motion starts a ripple that begins to spread out across the surface.

Our universe has existed for countless eons. Unimaginable trillions upon trillions of actions have hit that lake. These eons of cumulative actions, thoughts, and events forming waves and ripples and counter-waves reverberating in all directions, are still rippling through the foundation of nothingness.

This network of reverberating reactions crisscrossing each other in DO creates the fabric underlying our reality. This is the fabric that Lao Tzu calls "Heaven's Net."

"Heaven's net is ever large and wide.
Though its meshes are coarse, yet nothing slips through"

Tao Te Ching, Chapter 73

When he describes the mesh of the net of DO as coarse, he means it is invisible—as if the holes of this net are so big you can't see them and cannot even tell that you are caught in this net. In the case of heaven's net, even if there was a way out, how could we find it? There is no way we can escape it: We will always be inside of that net and subject to its action/reaction law.

Heaven's net is the analogy Lao Tzu uses for Dimension One. When Lao Tzu describes heaven's net as "ever large and wide," he is saying it is infinite in scope. Like that old Sunday school song, "So high you can't get over it, so low you can't get under it, so wide you can't get around it."

Since Dimension One is the foundation and building block of absolutely everything, it's everywhere. There is no such thing as being outside of DO. You can't be small enough to slip through it, you can't be big enough to smash it to bits, you can't step outside of it, there's nowhere you can run away to. You can't get out of that net! Nothing slips through.

Taoist sages spent their lifetimes observing the laws of action and reaction in human affairs, trying to understand the actions of this invisible net. Even though they couldn't see the net itself, they watched the *way* the net of DO worked. From what they saw, they left behind tips on how to take advantage of the power of heaven's net. They also warned how to avoid obstacles and tangles the net can pose to the unwary.

There are four important quotes in Eastern religion about heaven's net or "heaven's web." The first and fourth lines are from Lao Tzu, while the second and third are from Buddha. If we put them together in the following order, we have a complete and perfect picture of Dimension One—our word for heaven's net:

1. *Heaven's web, though invisible, is eternal and infinite in its immensity.*
2. *Everything is created by the oddness of that web action.*
3. *All actions are destined to ceaseless interactions.*
4. *Nothing escapes or parts from this invisible web.*

Let's take each quote one at a time and see if we can untangle more about Heaven's Net.

HEAVEN'S WEB, THOUGH INVISIBLE, IS ETERNAL AND INFINITE IN ITS IMMENSITY

Lao Tzu uses "heaven's net" to literally mean the ultimate fabric. Lao Tzu calls it the net. Buddha calls it thread or silk.

When we think of a net, we might visualize a fishing net woven of string or rope. However, a spider web might be a better analogy. Why? Because webs are sticky. If you walk through one, you can get tangled up, and the sticky pieces will either follow you or break off and stick to you if you manage to pull away.

Some spider webs are three-dimensional, extending in all directions—not just flat. Have you ever seen those spider webs that look like giant beehives or form curtains from the sky that look like clouds expanding in all directions? That's a better model of heaven's net: a sticky multidimensional web.

We talked about how atoms and molecules move so fast that they give the illusion of solid material like my desk. In the case of heaven's web, the waves and forces that make up its fabric aren't just spinning—they're moving in and out in every direction, so fast and so infinitely, they form the entire ocean of existence. That web extends everywhere.

"The Tao is invisible, but its power is infinite!
Though it appears unfathomable, it appears as if it is the source of the ten thousand things."

Tao Te Ching, Chapter 4

Part Four: The Net

Buddha and Lao Tzu often use the phrase "the 10,000 things" to describe everything that exists. But what they really mean is not only every physical thing, but also every event, every action, and every idea in the human mind.

They taught that the 10,000 things are born out of the action of that web. To them, space, stars, love, war, ghosts, and men, are all made from the same "stuff"—from the same origin. They all come out of the motion, the reverberations of heaven's net.

Every phenomenon, every event, and every "thing" is born out of this invisible web, made of this web, and moving inside this web. This makes it a dynamic web. It is moving all the time. Not only is it moving, but different pieces of it can appear and disappear in a moment. The web is flickering in and out of the nothingness since it's part of DO. That flicker speed is what makes it so hard to understand.

If I turn a light on and off fast enough, you would see a continuous, unbroken stream of light, even though it's not really continuous. Or if an airplane propeller spins fast enough, it can either look like a solid disk or look like it's not even there—even though both illusions aren't true. Likewise, our flickering DO can bring things in and out of reality, in and out of our awareness, in and out of visibility, making some things look stable and solid while hiding other things as invisible. It can be either something or nothing.

There's always a trick to analogies. For example, it's very easy to use a web or a net to understand how DO works, but there's no literal net or web. Don't confuse this with substance—it's still invisible and ultimately made of nothingness.

Since that web extends everywhere, through everyone, infinitely—it connects everything and everyone to everything else. We are all tied together by that web. We all connect!

But remember how a spiderweb works: If a fly steps on a spider web—on any thread, in any part of the web—the spider knows! How? The minute that fly steps on the web, it's connected to the spider. That spider's legs are touching the web and pick up any movement so that it can instantly travel along the web to catch and eat that fly.

Likewise, our every thought and action affect heaven's web. They send out a vibration through the web that anything and anyone can pick up. Anyone can pick up the vibrations from what we think and do because we're all touching that web.

That connection to everything and everyone is also how the consequences of our previous thoughts, words, and actions are able to find their way back to us, no matter how far away in space or time we've traveled.

In the case of our "heaven's web," there is an *internal web* and an *external web*. That's because we ourselves are made of that web *and* walking around in a world made of DO as well. That's why we don't even have to act to trigger that web action—we just have to think, and the internal piece of the web we carry around can pick that up and send that signal to the entire external web.

It's not so much a "web that has no weaver." It's more accurate to say that everything and everyone is a weaver, and we are continually weaving the very net that entangles us. We play both the spider and the fly. We are all continually acting and thinking and saying things that reverberate in that invisible network. Every thought, word, or action adds another thread to the web. That thread will stick to us and pull in the automatic consequences of whatever we wove. And we will unconsciously be pulled to others in reaction to what they've done or said.

Much of the old Buddhist and Taoist wisdom was how to touch that net safely and not trigger bad reactions. The reason that a Taoist can see the past and future or know what others are thinking is that they've learned to feel, sense, and see with DO power and can connect to that piece of heaven's net deep inside of themselves and pick up the information like a spider on a web.

Lao Tzu was one of those old spiders. He could access DO and took pains to describe heaven's net so we could learn what he learned. He answers the question, "What is DO?" and "What is the nature of that DO space?" Lao Tzu says the net is very soft, weak, refined, not noticeable. Here's his description of heaven's net:

"Look, but you cannot see it —it is formless.
Listen, but you cannot hear it—it transcends sound.
Grasp, but you can hold nothing—it is intangible.
These three are unfathomable.
Therefore, they are merged as one.
From above it reflects no light; from below it casts no shadow.
Impossible to comprehend, it cannot be named.
Eventually it returns to nothingness.
So it is called a form without form, a shape without shape.
It is called vague and subtle.
Encounter it from the front and you can't see its head.

*Follow after it and you can't see its back.
Hold onto the ancient origin as you deal with the present.
Knowing the origin is the law of Tao."*

Tao Te Ching, Chapter 14

This seems more like nonsense! But this is Lao Tzu describing DO space and its ultimate rules.

He then goes on to describe how to train yourself to live in that DO space. Here's how a master walks on that web:

*"The ancient masters were subtle, mysterious, profound,
and aware.
The extreme depth of their knowledge is hard to understand.
Since they are unfathomable, allow me to try very hard
to describe their appearance in this way:
Watchful, just like crossing a winter stream.
Ever alert, like aware of surrounding danger.
Courteous, like facing very important guests.
Yielding, like ice about to melt.
Appearing so simple and real,
like an uncarved block of wood.
So hollow and deep, like a big canyon.
Resting, won't the mud settle and the water
become clear again?
Can't he rest knowing that stillness will again
awaken into action?
Knowing the way of the Tao, he never seeks to be full.
Never full, even the worn-out need not be renewed."*

Tao Te Ching, Chapter 15

When we're just beginning, we can't know what it feels like to know what Taoists know. Just like I cannot know how it really feels to be inside a cat's body, what their neurological experience is like. I can only describe a cat's movements. Lao Tzu can only describe how a Taoist master looks to us from the outside.

Most people can't feel that web. It takes time and training to learn how. Until then, you're still learning what the laws are here in DO space. If you enter a new environment and you don't know the rules and laws, you're at a bigger risk for danger.

That's why those old Buddhist and Taoists left a helpful list of rules we can use. They help us while we're bumbling around in that web, so we don't get tangled up or draw in spiders.

In today's world, we have a transportation network that looks like a net. It's a surface web we call roadways. I can take my car on that network any time I like, and if I follow the traffic laws, I'll be okay. If we all take turns at stop signs and drive in our own lanes, then you and I won't collide with each other or other vehicles.

Likewise, in the network of heaven's web, if I follow certain laws like "do not kill," "do not steal," "do not lie," I'll be okay. I won't twist that web in the wrong way so that it brings in bad spiders. I can stay more nimble, less stuck. More importantly, I won't have killing, stealing, and lying rebounding back at me in the future. Those rules are there to help me stay safe.

Following the rules not only wards off danger, but it can create a happier place to be. On the roadway, if we contribute to an overarching culture of good drivers, we learn to value being polite to each other. We let faster drivers pass, we let others cut in, we take turns in a merge lane, and stay patient in a traffic jam. This culture makes for safer travel and an enjoyable trip for everyone.

On heaven's network, I know that if I can throw good thoughts and kind actions at that rebounding net, these will come back to me through the assurance of that rule. If we have a culture of everyone doing the same gentle and kind actions, everything will get better over time.

EVERYTHING IS CREATED BY THE ODDNESS OF THAT WEB ACTION

Because our actions and their resounding reactions continue to bombard us, crisscrossing with everyone else's actions and reactions, the net is always throbbing, always reverberating, always producing change.

DO stays the same. Water is always just water. But its surface, that net that forms our reality, is constantly changing. The waves never stand still.

If I am unconscious or dead and just floating on the water, I cause no waves. But if I slightly awaken and twitch my finger, even just a little bit, it will launch a tiny wave that will eventually move outward and touch you. Once that small wave touches you, it will rebound and cause another small wave that starts flowing back to me. If we are all swimming and thrashing around in the water, soon the surface becomes crossed in countless directions by waves upon waves. The compounded waves from our actions and reactions in the water become a churning, interweaving network of wakes, waves, and tides. This wild and wavy surface of DO is the very fabric of the world we live in. It's what we are made of.

These waves also form what we call karma—they bombard and rebound all over to become that fabric, that network. But because there are so many swimmers in the water and so many actions continually rebounding, the wave patterns are disorganized, complicated—less predictable.

If I do something bad, like steal, I don't always feel the repercussions right away. It can seem that there is no bad effect from stealing. Not seeing any repercussions, I go right on stealing, unaware that eventually I'll get punished by that rebound effect. Sure enough, though, at some point, I'll get caught and punished, or someone else will steal from me. Most likely, it will happen when I least expect it!

So, when Buddha says: "Everything is created by the *oddness* of that web action," he means that our own actions and their inevitable repercussions don't happen predictably.

The reason I'm not punished right away is why Buddha calls it odd. The action/reaction of karma isn't predictable and cannot be timed because our actions and consequences intersect with so many other people's actions and consequences, as well our own actions still reverberating from the past. That oddness is why Buddha also advised that we can never know when a good or bad deed will bear fruit, but that it certainly will over time.

That oddness is also why everything we know is in a constant state of change. Our universe is always subtly changing. It's all one flowing piece that is continually moving. It's like that old adage, "You can never step in the same river twice."

Yet, in this case, we are part of that river—we ride right on top of it. Because it is ever-flowing, and because we ride on top of it, we are forced to flow with it. Like it or not, we are carried through change after change after change.

Time itself is always changing. It never stops and stays still. You can never truly be in "right now" because there is no such thing. If you ask, "What's right now?" the answer is "Changing." Everything is always in one of three states: before change, during change, and after change.

The Taoists learned skills that helped them adapt to change with greater harmony and without resistance. For example, when the water is full of waves or rushing rapids, sometimes you can survive better if you relax and float. When you relax and take things as they come, you can ride on top of the rough water and flow with the current, rather than be overcome or drowned by swimming against the tide.

Likewise, in our lives, when things are turbulent, sometimes it's best to calm down, slow down, and go with the flow, rather than franticly thrash around. Chances are, if we just stay calm, the flow of events will take us right where we need to go.

If action is called for, you can use DO to sense what's coming next. It lets you read the water ahead and see where the rocks are before they come so that you can try to steer around them. Being calm and adapting to change allow us to take right action, to steer around the rocks in our lives, not just react to bad events, hurtful words, or trouble. If we react, it's like we keep bouncing off one rock only to collide with another.

One thing is for sure: change is inevitable, so to not expect or adapt to change is a big mistake.

Change is part of the oddness of that net. The river of change is the river of rebounding reverberations of heaven's net as it throbs and weaves what we've thought and done over time back to us.

As sure as the Sun will rise, even if we cannot time it or predict it, if we have ever done wrong or hurt someone, lied, stolen, or killed, the rebound effects will eventually find us—even if it's decades or even lifetimes later. This is why Buddhists say, "You never know when a good deed or a bad deed will bear fruit." In that way, the net is odd, but it's very dependable.

The consequences of your action may not be right away and often take quite a while due to the oddness of that net. For that reason, we tend to forget about that net when we act. This is why those same religions gave us reminders like: "What you sow, you shall also reap." "Cast your bread out on the water, and you will find it in many days." "Do unto others as you would have done unto you." They're actually saying, "Slow down! Don't forget about that net!" Those warnings weren't meant to be dogma; they were science lessons learned by years of observation.

ALL ACTIONS ARE DESTINED TO CEASELESS INTERACTIONS

What Buddha concluded was the same thing Sir Isaac Newton and science observed: every action has equal and opposite reaction. But Buddha took it a step further to say: *"All actions are destined to ceaseless interactions."*

We can model the ceaseless nature of action/reaction with that old desktop toy that offers a line of suspended steel marbles. If you swing one marble to hit the other marbles, it causes the opposite marble to swing and hit the line again, causing the first marble to once again swing and clack, and on and on, click-clack, until it gradually slows and eventually stops.

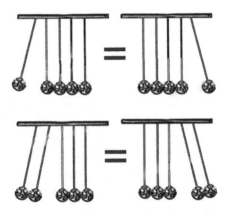

If you've ever played with one of these toys, you know that there are endless patterns of action/reactions that you can create from swinging marbles in different rhythms and sequences. You can swing two balls on one end, and two balls on the opposite end will move. Whatever rhythms and sequences you set in motion will keep going and going until their energy dissipates and the whole toy goes back into stillness.

When Buddha observes that "all actions are destined to ceaseless interactions," he's saying the ramifications of everything we do and everything that happens vibrates and echoes back to us, not just once, but over and over again, potentially forever. That includes both physical and non-physical actions.

That means our universe is much like that desk toy. But instead of five marbles clacking in a line, our "universal desk toy" has infinite "marbles" clacking in infinite directions.

While we are alive, we continue to move, think, speak and act. That means we continually set into action more ceaseless reactions whether we want to or not. It's virtually impossible not to. We're always creating more waves, which create others, ad infinitum.

This action and reaction phenomenon is a truth of DO. It's the truth that underlies what we would call the Taoist's view of "creation." One action creates another and another and, ultimately, the 10,000 things.

*"The Tao created the One. The One flows into two.
The two generate the three.
The three generate the 10,000 things."*

Tao Te Ching, Chapter 42

Our own ability to think is a piece of DO inside of us. That's why everything we do is a microcosm of creation. Like DO, everything begins in the stillness of our mind. Our mind creates a single thought. That thought moves us into action. That action then breeds a series of reactions. 1 -2 -3 →→ 10,000.

When you played with that desk toy, what was your first action? Actually, your first action was thinking, "Hey, look, a desk toy—I'm going to go play with it." Your first action was a thought, and then after that thought, you swung the first marble. Every second and subsequent clack is a child of that first thought just as much as it is of that first marble.

If I initiate a thought, and that thought prompts me to act, it's as if I put a seed in the ground. That seed will first grow a tree, then that tree will bear fruit. Once this tree grows a fruit, that fruit will bear a seed, that seed will grow into another tree, that tree will bear fruit, and that cycle will continue and keep going. It's the ceaseless chain of reactions I set in motion after planting that first seed.

That's the same with thoughts and actions. If I take an action, there will be another action that comes in response, and then that action will lead to another—ultimately producing several generations of actions.

But is that how it really works? Do I plant a seed, which grows a tree, which bears a fruit with another seed?

No! That tree will bear *hundreds* of fruits, and each fruit can have a dozen or more seeds. So it not only creates one linear generation of reactions, but those reactions amplify and expand, radiating outward exponentially. If we plant one seed and walk away for a few years, when we come back, a whole forest of fruit trees could stand in its place, not just one.

Likewise, the chain reaction started by your action isn't just linear; it also radiates outward and can be far-reaching, just like one seed can produce a whole forest of fruit trees.

That's why those old masters were calm and cautious, ever alert. They knew that just one wrong thought or action could set in motion an endless and far-reaching cycle of events.

Part Four: The Net

Lao Tzu warns:

"Regard the small as if it were large, and the few as if it were many . . .
Plan for difficulties while a situation is still simple to solve.
Act on big things while they are still small.
In the universe, difficult things start out easy.
In the universe, large things arise from the small."

Tao Te Ching, Chapter 63

If Lao Tzu could steal a more modern cliché, he'd tell us that if you see that you've planted the wrong seed and trouble is growing, then "nip it in the bud."

It's also why Lao Tzu advises:

"It is easy to maintain a situation while it is still at peace.
Plan for change before it happens.
While still weak, it is easy to shatter.
While still small, it is easily scattered.
Act on it before it happens.
Create order before it becomes chaos.
A tree so big that it takes many men to embrace it starts from a tiny shoot.
A nine-story terrace starts with a bucket of earth.
A journey of a thousand miles starts beneath one's feet."

Tao Te Ching, Chapter 64

We like to use Lao Tzu's famous quote to encourage each other at new beginnings, saying: "The journey of a thousand miles starts with just one step!" But what we also need to understand is that the journey of a thousand miles in the wrong direction also starts with just one step. Lao Tzu is warning us to go slowly and carefully, knowing that the smallest action can be amplified into big consequences due to the laws of heaven's net.

As human beings in a complex world of suffering and confusion, we often spend our lives searching for the truth. But in our search, we often stop at just the surface level.

My friend John walks up to me and kicks my leg for what seems like no reason. I might get mad at John and kick him back. That might start a fight with John. That plants a bad seed that could grow a forest of trouble for both John and me. We could keep fighting and hurt each other or even end up arrested. We could hate each other for the rest of our lives. Those bad actions and hurt feelings will just keep going and going.

Instead, I'm smart. I don't kick back. Instead, I wonder, "Why did John kick my leg? Maybe it's because I owe him $20 and haven't paid him back." So instead of kicking him, I ask him, "Hey, John! Why did you kick me? Are you mad because I still owe you $20?"

When I try to find a reason why John kicked me, I'm looking for the parent, the seed, or the original source that caused his action. I want to get back to the root so we can solve our problem once and for all, so it doesn't happen again.

But I can keep going backward: Why did I need to borrow $20 from John in the first place? Ah, because I lost my job. Why did I lose my job? Oh, because I called the boss an idiot and embarrassed him in front of his wife. I now see that the *root* of my problem goes further back than just owing John money.

Any tree you pick in the woods came from millions of generations of previous trees. If you could trace it, at some point, that tree's lineage goes all the way back to the very first tree and the very first seed from the very first fruit.

To find the truth in any situation, we have to go back many steps: first to find the cause, and then the cause of that cause, and the cause of that cause, and finally back to the first action that initiated the string of events.

There are regions in our world where conflict erupts again and again. The Middle East comes to mind. There are hot spots of war in Asia, Africa, and Eastern Europe as well. Tribe A kills Tribe B. But that's because, in the last generation, Tribe B killed Tribe A. If you go back another century, Tribe A was killing tribe B. It goes on like this for centuries. You can trace the historical roots of that region's conflict almost to the beginning of mankind's written history. But what about before written history? They were still fighting, most likely.

Everything that happens to us is a result of a line of actions planted along the way. But as human beings, I can only trace an event's cause back so far. At some point, I lose the thread of how it all started.

Even if there is no written record or human memory of what originally started a conflict, the cause is always recorded in heaven's net. It preserves that record like an echo that goes on forever. Because it preserves that record, that's why we can never escape the repercussions of our actions and why they will always find us again.

But thanks to that same record in heaven's net, highly achieved Taoists can see that chain of events that marks the truth of any situation. It's as if they can look at a seed and see all the way back to the very first tree.

What is the core of this ability? DO! Since DO is the origin of all that exists, and since DO connects to and through everything, by touching DO, the Taoist master has access to a vast encyclopedia. He can pull the record of the entire series of events leading to any given situation. He can see the "lineage" of cause and effect behind each event and each person.

When I can see things from the higher dimension of DO, then I can see and understand everything. On Earth, it took human beings a long time to map our planet with its continents and oceans. We were stuck in our Earth dimension and had to use complex math, scopes, and tools to trace every coastline. But once we went higher and could fly a spaceship above the Earth, suddenly, we could confirm it is round and that the shapes of the continents on my wall map are correct. I don't need math or a compass. From my spaceship, I can take in the whole real view in one glance.

In DO, I can see why John gets mad at me and kicks me because I have access to John's dimension and can see all the causes that lead up to that action in just one glance. At a human level, I cannot see that. On the human level, I only have sciences like psychology or sociology to figure out why John kicks people when he's mad. But I can never know the real cause until I upgrade to DO science and see the situation from a higher level.

NOTHING ESCAPES OR PARTS FROM THIS INVISIBLE WEB

One reason you cannot escape this net is it follows you wherever you go. The threads of this net behave like chewing gum on the bottom of your shoe. As soon as you step on it, it clings, stretches, and pulls, and now that thread of chewing gum is following you everywhere you go.

DO chewing gum, however, is different than the kind I buy at the drugstore. DO chewing gum follows me even if I travel 10,000 miles away. It also follows me through time and space. A year or more has passed and the chewing gum still follows. I try to get it off, and then it sticks to my fingers. The nature of this chewing gum ensures that my destiny is sealed, that whatever reaction or consequence I've created will always be able to find me.

There are two problems with this chewing gum that make up heaven's net: (1) It's infinite with no limit, and (2) It's invisible. If it were visible, you might be able to manage it so that you didn't touch any more chewing gum, or you could slowly manage to scrape it off or unwind it so that the gum didn't entangle you as much.

Another way heaven's net is inescapable is that it is round. How do we know it is round? By the part of it we *can* see.

Scientists calculate the shape and expanding motion of the universe and describe it as curved or round. It seems to be continually curving in upon itself. The most natural and powerful shapes we find in the universe are also round. Galaxies are round, stars and planets are round, atoms and particles are round, even human life begins from one single cell, which is round.

Roundness is a characteristic of DO's cyclical nature. Why? Because of the action of Neng and Kong. Everything is moving in a cycle or circle as it goes outward through the action of Neng and then coming back to stillness through the returning nature of Kong. Through Neng and Kong, DO constantly moves outward toward action, then returns to rest. Out and return. Out and return. Inward and outward, again and again.

Lao Tzu describes DO's round nature and how it is always moving out toward the far away only to return:

Something mysteriously formed, born even before heaven and earth;
In the loneliness and the void, standing alone and unchanging,
Ever present and moving ceaselessly. It is the mother of heaven and earth.
I do not know its name. Let's just call it Tao.
For lack of a better word, let's call it the Great.
So great, let's call it disappearing.
Disappearing into far away—let's call it the far away.
Having gone so far, eventually it returns—so let's call it the return.

Tao Te Ching, Chapter 25

And in another chapter, Lao Tzu says simply:

"The Tao moves toward the direction of returning."

Tao Te Ching, Chapter 40

In another section, he describes what he sees in meditation when he touches DO. He sees all existence appearing in a circular sequence and then returning to stillness.

"Attain to the utmost inward weakness.
Focus firmly in the purest state of stillness.
Suddenly, the 10,000 things will appear in
circular sequence.
And then everything will develop and flourish
and then return to the source of the void.
Returning to the source is the stillness.

Tao Te Ching, Chapter 16

DO's roundness and its cycle of creation and return are why so many phenomena in nature also rise and fall in circular cycles: they follow the master pattern of the universe. You can see that cycle's pattern in the circle of the seasons, the rotation of the hours of the day, our sleeping and waking cycle, the water cycle of evaporation and rain, the circulation of our blood through the heart, our breath as we inhale and exhale. Everything rises upward into full activity and then returns to rest—only to start another cycle.

The roundness of the cycles within life and nature aren't the only ways the returning nature of DO expresses itself. The roundness of heaven's net is precisely the reason why we can never escape the consequences of our actions.

Because of DO's roundness, it's as if we are living in an enclosure. If you traveled along the inner or outer surface of a sphere, you'd just keep going around and around.

Your travel never really ends anywhere, as there is no edge or corner, no finish line, no way out. Eventually, you'll always wind up at the same place you started. That's why in DO, everything keeps coming around again. It can't go anywhere else.

Take the roundness of our planet: If you dump radioactive waste or tsunami debris into the ocean, it won't disappear. It will always be stuck in the round container that is our planet. The ocean current will simply flow the debris around and around, perhaps depositing it in California or Alaska or bring it around to Japan's shores. Garbage cannot escape the enclosure of our planet. We think we are throwing things away, but there is no "away" in a round container.

If I dump some bad stuff in an enclosure, too bad; I can't get away. But it's worse than that. Not only is our container round, but it's always moving and changing. If a cat pees in the corner of your apartment, you can still smell it anywhere you go, but you can at least go in another room where you don't have to look at it or step in it. But imagine if your apartment floor is always moving in a circle while you go about your business. In that case, if your cat pees, eventually that cat pee will come and touch you and even touch the cat again just by the law of odds.

Action inside the roundness of heaven's net is like being locked inside a steel silo with a gun. Every bullet you fire keeps ricocheting around. That bullet will ricochet around and around and eventually come back and hit you.

In the round enclosure of DO, everything you send out will ultimately come back to you, including your thoughts and deeds. No human action, tangible or intangible, can escape this law. It must come back to you. The only question is how and when.

You run here, you run there, but you can never get away. There is no escape. That's why in life, it can sometimes seem like you are going in a circle, running on a hamster wheel. You get hit by the same type of problems, the same conundrums, the same type of relationships, over and over and over. This is because that net is still vibrating and returning or reverberating back to you an echo of what you've sent out in the past. It has nowhere else to go, and it's what was attached to your chewing gum!

Every action you take, every thought, has consequences that return to you just like the law of relativity in a silo. It's how the roundness of DO reinforces karma. When you think or act, your thought and action happen through the power of DO and inside of DO and register as events within heaven's net. Those thoughts and actions become part of a round, rebounding framework that guarantees the return of everything to its origin. This is why "what goes around, comes around," "what you sow, you shall reap," or "we are punished by our own actions."

Some societies observed that since bad actions resulted in bad consequences so reliably and good behavior resulted in blessing so often, reward and punishment must be disseminated by supernatural divinities or gods. Whether you believe in such gods or not, the reactions and consequences of karma follow the same principles that make a ball roll or a wheel spin or our planet orbit the Sun. Our thoughts and actions are contained in a circular system that ultimately cycles everything through and back to its source.

We cannot escape the consequences of our actions because of the roundness of that net. But also, *we cannot escape that net because we ourselves are made of that net.*

If I try to escape, try to cut or sever myself from that net—think my own way, be my own boss, chase my own agenda—I will meet with disaster. That's what Lao Tzu means in the *Tao Te Ching* Chapter 73 when he says, *"If one is simply brave and daring, he will be killed."*

Being very brave by trying to cut ourselves off that net and running away from the consequences of our actions or reversing them with brute force is like pulling a rubber band. The rubber band will simply snap back and hurt us. If I try to sever myself and move away from DO, I can never escape because I'm always connected to it. I'm part of the rubber band. So instead of escaping, I can only snap back into place through the law of cause and effect.

Our lack of awareness of the truth that we are all connected by heaven's net is the foundation of our ignorance. It's why we feel cut off and separate when we aren't. This ignorance is why we keep making things worse for ourselves and why we wrongfully think of ourselves as separate from other people and the consequences we create when we hurt others.

If just one soul is suffering, we all suffer. If one person has a wicked and nasty idea, everybody suffers because we all come from the same origin and live in the same silo.

If one person suffers, then everyone suffers. Why? Because this person will come back in another life with a claim on his or her right to avenge that suffering and start the whole process over. And they will find you easily if you caused their suffering. The record is there in that net, and that chewing gum leads back to you.

Part Four: The Net

We are all pulling on the same rubber band. You cannot get away. I cannot get away. Nobody can escape that invisible net. All of humanity is part of that net. We cannot even escape this net by dying.

Death is something we greatly misunderstand as a result of our limited thinking. It's another cycle of coming and going, entering and returning. It's part of a circle that has no beginning and no end. The minute we think beginning and end, we have the false concept of birth and death.

When you die, you simply change zones, just like you change zones when you go to sleep. The you of you never changes: it's you in the zone before birth, you when you wake up and live here in the human zone, you when you sleep and go to the dream zone, and you when you die and go to a different zone.

But no matter what zone we travel to, no matter how much time lapses, we are still always and ever in that net, enclosed in that big silo, and our consequences find us.

DO IS LIKE A GONG

Another analogy to understand how DO works is to think of it as a large gong. What are the characteristics of a gong? If you don't hit a gong, it makes no sound. If you hit it lightly, it makes a soft sound. If you hit it hard, it makes a very loud sound. A gong broadcasts a resounding clang that matches the force hitting it.

Imagine if you were told that there was an invisible gong in an otherwise empty room. To find it, you'd need to swing a mallet in several spots around the room. Eventually, by trial and error, you'd hit that invisible gong.

Once you hit that invisible gong, its vibration and sound will radiate outward. Once it reverberates, it's no longer invisible—we know the gong is there by its sound.

The gong we call DO is also invisible. We can't see, feel, or hear it, but it's everywhere. But any time we act or think, it is like hitting that invisible gong. Once we hit it, it reverberates in kind—so even if it's invisible, by its reverberation, we know that it's there. We see the way it works by its effects on our lives.

In chapter 79 of the *Tao Te Ching*, Lao Tzu tells us more about how DO works like a gong. He says that *"Tao is fair, impartial, showing preference to no one, but it always blesses a good man."*

What does this mean? How can it be impartial but always bless someone who is good? Isn't that showing favoritism instead of impartiality?

No, it's not. Let's dissect what Lao Tzu is saying because he's explaining how that DO gong works.

Let's say we act, we think, or we ask something. We hit that DO "gong." That gong sends back an answer. It doesn't matter what we hit it with; it will answer in kind to whatever we hit it with.

If we hit that gong with bad stuff—anger, jealousy, and revenge—it will send back that same message. Equally, if we hit that gong with good stuff—love, blessing, and gratitude—it will send back that same message as well. That is what makes this gong "fair" and "impartial." It will send back whatever you send out to it.

This is also why it "always blesses a good man." A good man is always sending out an action, an intention, and a thought of goodness. He hits that gong with goodness, so goodness is what reverberates back to him. But because DO is impartial, it will also send and reflect back what is bad to the person of wrong action, bad thought, and ill intent.

In that way, we could say that DO is also like a mirror, reflecting back to us what we show it, a likeness of our own energy, mind, and intentions.

Yet a gong is a much better analogy than a mirror. Why? Because a mirror only sends a two-dimensional reflection back, but a gong can amplify sound and send it out in all directions.

When you hit that gong of DO, you get back whatever is in the nature of your action, thought, or intent. DO is neither good nor bad in and of itself. It doesn't judge. It merely reflects back or amplifies what you are sending out. In respect to DO, you suit yourself by what you choose to be, think, and do. If you hit that gong with a bad message, what you receive in return will come back with a bad message.

When the *Tao Te Ching* says DO "blesses" those who do good, blesses a good man, it only appears as if Tao is blessing that person. DO doesn't necessarily choose to bless; it is that good person that is receiving an amplification of what they send out in good thoughts, deeds, actions, intentions, and prayers. It would be more accurate to say that it is *you yourself* who hit that gong, and as a result, you caused your own blessing.

But you cannot just decide to bless yourself; you need to hit that gong. You need that gong action to get that amplification effect in your life.

It is very hard to hit the gong of DO directly and effectively. Our good deeds and good intentions are often hit or miss. Why? Our artificial, detached version of thinking and our insincerity block a direct hit. Our everyday mental activity and actions are very artificial and weak. We can't hit that gong with enough force to cause a strong reverberation. That's why our best efforts at "think and receive" or "create your own reality" or "put that positive thought out into the universe" often deliver results that fall far short of our expectations. Our affirmations and visualizations are too hollow to hit that gong with a force strong enough to produce strong results. It's as if the mallet we are using is covered in wads of cotton so thick; no matter how hard we try, we cannot get much sound out of that gong.

The mallet we hit that gong with is our mind. To really hit that gong, you need a *pure* mind, sincere intentions, and a clarity that most human beings have lost. We need to unwrap that mallet from the many layers of insulation and then learn how to aim that mallet at the gong's center to produce results. That's another goal the Taoists worked toward: amplifying DO's action/reaction power to their advantage. To do that, they unwrapped their mallet—they purified their minds and focused their intention to the utmost. They did this through lifestyle, moving meditation, and practice.

Those Taoists learned how to aim the mallet of their mind straight to the center of DO. A centered hit like that can produce instantaneous results. It's the root of the "miracles" or answered prayer Taoist masters could affect.

What makes us ineffective in hitting that gong today? The more attachments, desires, agendas, and purposes behind my good deeds and thoughts, the further away I am from directly hitting that gong to receive good in return. Oh, it may have some effect, but I won't activate the potential in DO. Instead of hitting the gong full-on in the sweet center spot, I'll maybe just scrape the edge getting only a weak, tinny, and grating sound.

For example, can I hold no ulterior motives when I do a good deed? If I only put money in a beggar's bucket to get the approval of everyone who's watching, that's a miss. If I say nice words to someone because I want them to vote for me when I run for the school board, that's a miss.

We don't understand why we seem to receive only bitterness or mediocre results in our lives, despite our prayers, meditations, and practice. It's because we are not hitting that gong with true, sincere good thought or deed, or we are hitting it with bad ones whether we realize it or not. We think our prayer for a new luxury car is "good," but we may not identify the notes of selfishness, greed, a false sense of need, or our desire to impress others that take us off the mark. We miss that gong or get a result we didn't expect.

When you understand the law of DO's rebound and return power, the power of that gong, and set out to "use" the power or DO for your own benefit, you might instead send out ego, selfishness, greed, or ingratitude to that gong. Positive thinking and affirmations and certainly working hard to lead a good life are a great signal to send out to that gong—however, you may not be calculating everything going into the mix.

We also don't calculate our past actions. Although you may be a good person and a positive thinker today, that gong is still sending back bad stuff you hit it with years ago or perhaps even before this lifetime. If you've ever hit a gong, you know it can take several minutes for the sound to completely die down. If you're working hard to be a sincere and good person, but you're seeing no results, chances are the "sound" of your old self hasn't died down in that gong just yet.

When people try hard to be positive and helpful, sometimes they are still met with suffering. This can cause many to lose heart and give up or believe that the laws of cause and effect aren't real. Perseverance at right thinking and right behavior are important.

Understanding more about how DO works helps you gain that perseverance and stay the course and hit that gong the right way. To do that, you need to immerse yourself in the study of DO science.

PART FIVE

DO SCIENCE

*"Thirty spokes share a wheel's hub, but it's the center hole
that makes it useful for a vehicle.
Mold clay into a pot; it is the hollow space within
that makes it a useful vessel.
Cut out doors and windows of a room; it is the enclosed
space that makes it useful as a house.
Therefore, to benefit from having something, one must also
employ having nothing to achieve its usefulness."*

Tao Te Ching, Chapter 11

UNTANGLING THE NET: THE SCIENCE OF DO

That sticky nature of the net, the net that follows us wherever we go, brings so many difficulties to our door. Strings from the net can tangle up like a fishing line. We get drawn into controversies and complicated relationships that seem impossible to resolve. They are caused by an inescapable tangle of actions and reactions we've been a part of over many lifetimes.

To untangle that net in our lives, reduce suffering and the consequences of our past, and to lay a course for a better future for ourselves is the science of DO. It's the science that Jesus, Buddha, and Lao Tzu studied and what you're learning in this book.

For example, Buddha says, when you initiate action, it will yield the return of ceaseless counteraction. Does that mean we are forever doomed if we make a mistake and act badly? How can we reduce the tidal waves of reactions to our past misdeeds or quiet that net so that we can lessen our suffering and the suffering of others?

The DO science in Buddhism and Taoism offers several answers. One answer is to simply not think so much. That's why they gave us so many teachings to reduce our thinking and thus reduce our actions. They wanted us to simplify our lives and quiet our minds.

Why reduce our thinking? Because one worry leads to three worries, then four, then five. Thoughts can also lead to actions; then, the chain reactions are almost impossible to stop.

Thought #1:
"Property taxes are due next month."

Thought #2:
"How the heck am I going to pay my taxes?"

Thought #3:
"I hate this town and its high taxes."

Thought #4:
"If I made more money, I could pay my taxes."

Thought #6:
"I should rob a bank like John told me. Ha-ha-ha."

Thought #7:
"I wonder how hard it is to rob a bank? John said it was actually easy."

Action:
Calls John and laughs about robbing a bank. But John is serious and wants to get together to discuss a plan. They meet for lunch. A thousand thoughts and a few actions later, they rob a bank.

To intervene and stop the chain of thoughts, we have to work on stopping the first thought. How can I have no first thought? That's impossible because our mind never stops!

If I can't stop thinking, how can I discipline my mind and steer my thoughts in a more positive direction? That's why many Eastern and Western religions came up with 37 ways to reduce thinking: They want you to distract your mind with chanting, prayer, Zen meditation, singing, etc. Part of why these practices work so well is they occupy your mind and give you something to focus on that's neutral or positive and less likely to lead to bad thoughts.

Another tactic is to teach you to reduce your judgments about what is good or bad so that you don't automatically react with fear or anger. Or they encourage you to spend more time in kind actions and good deeds.

These are all ways based in DO science to reduce or eliminate new chains of ceaseless negative reactions.

Those old sages discovered that sneaking around and tiptoeing on that net is the best approach. Once you set that net into motion, you can guarantee it will yield an endless return of counteraction, and back into the never-ending mess you go!

Jesus had an even more clever way to deal with the rebound reactions of that net. He said, *"If someone hits you on the cheek, turn your other cheek and let him hit the other side too."* Or, *"If someone steals your shirt, give him your coat, too."* Or even *"love your enemy."*

This advice goes beyond cultivating good and kind behavior or receiving a wrong graciously. Jesus asks us to *overcompensate*!

What he discovered is that when someone hurts you, most likely it is a reaction to previous hurt you did to them, whether you remember it or not. If you react yet *again* in violence, you are only reinforcing the momentum of that endless rebounding of violence in heaven's net.

But, if you refuse to react with violence, it's as if you've surrounded your steel marble with a big wad of cotton. Now that desk toy won't clack as loudly. The rebound of future violence won't be as strong. The pattern of violence and rebounding violence that was set in motion in the past will wind itself down faster or perhaps dissipate altogether if you're lucky.

Part Five: DO Science

If you go even *further*, like Jesus says, and not only refuse to react negatively but instead react *proactively* with forgiveness or kindness, that can buffer whatever rebounding actions come back to you in the future. Furthermore, if you *overcompensate* and allow that guy to hit *both* cheeks, to steal *both* your shirt and your coat, it has an even greater effect at calming the endless subsequent reactions of heaven's net. By giving that thief your coat *now* instead of rebuking him or having him arrested, you might stop him from stealing 100 shirts from you in the *future*.

The big takeaway from Jesus' teaching of turning the other cheek and loving your enemies is this: How you react to wrongs done against you will be the flavor of what comes back to you down the road, endlessly. And, most importantly, *you can affect the quality of that rebound now by your actions.* You can quiet tomorrow's storm today.

Jesus' teaching had little to do with "morals" and everything to do with the applied science of DO. Likewise, major laws found in most religions, like "do not kill" or "do not steal," are not simply moral issues. They are sound science based on the observation of that action/reaction principle.

Likewise, Buddha's teaching about quieting desires and emotions wasn't a moral teaching: If I am greedy, if I lie, if I fear, get jealous, nasty, afraid, very happy, very sad, it can put me at risk with heaven's net. The reason these are not allowed has nothing to do with morality. It's because we worry about setting that action/reaction principle in motion. It's DO science. Strong emotions disturb our calm and often prod us to act, and often to act badly. Strong emotions and bad thoughts can also subtly trigger that net.

Most religions also tell us to do good to others. They advise us to seek opportunities to be helpful, compassionate, and kind in addition to doing no harm. It can seem like simple wisdom, but the DO effect is powerful. Remember, your actions create their own 10 thousand or 10 trillion ceaseless reactions. They all keep going. What do you want to set in motion for yourself and the world?

Those sages also believed that some of these reactions could cancel each other out. If you send out enough good into the world, it can intercept and smooth out the waves of hurt and harm heading toward you. Those waves of good and bad crash into each other and lose their momentum.

Forgiving and letting go are also other ways we can soften the blows that are on their way toward us. We can learn to let many of our problems, disagreements, or judgments about other people go. When we let go of the need to defend ourselves, elevate ourselves, prove something, or get revenge, we are quieting that net using DO science.

DO SCIENCE IS MULTIDIMENSIONAL

The great thing about becoming a DO scientist is that it applies universally to every part of our lives and to every possible dimension.

Unfortunately, most human level science doesn't apply to other dimensions, and it certainly doesn't apply to DO. Our human science only applies to the limited dimension of the immediate universe that we can perceive with our human senses and human calculations. As soon as we move out of our own dimension, our science doesn't work. Different dimensions have different rules.

Different dimensions aren't necessarily eerie or mysterious. But it's important to know about them and how they can affect each other.

A dog or cat can live in your apartment, but they hear different things and smell different things than you hear or smell. It's as if they live in a different dimension than you do. However, your dimension and the dog's dimension intersect in that apartment because you are sharing the same space. Your dimensions affect each other. If you hide all the food and water and never let him outside, that dog might die. If that dog gets angry enough, he might bite you. If you are good to each other and forge a friendship, you can help and protect each other. The two of you can reach across the dimensions to help or hurt each other because your dimensions intersect. Because your dimensions overlap—you can change each other's reality.

Likewise, in your apartment, there may be many other invisible dimensions you cannot see. Even though they are invisible to us, they can still affect us. For example, the waves that deliver cell phone calls and television signals are surrounding you in your apartment. You can't see or perceive them unless you tune into them with your phone or TV. When you tune into them with the correct device, the information they carry can vastly change your dimension. How? They can change your thinking and change your views about the world.

As human beings, our body is like our apartment. We have dimensions of ourselves that we can see and feel and dimensions of ourselves that we can't. The part of us that is made of heaven's net is invisible. But just because we can't see it doesn't mean it isn't constantly affecting us. And like our dog or cat, it's a part of us that can sense things that our thinking mind or five senses can't.

That invisible part of us also picks up what we consciously can't about other people and situations. It's the part of us that draws in and attracts people that might be either good for us or bad for us. It knows and identifies people connected to us by "karma." The word karma can carry some religious baggage in its interpretation, but in DO science, karma is simply the inerasable record of our past action/reactions that's embedded in heaven's net. It's like an invisible "beeper" we carry with us at all times. It sends out a signal over that network so that others can find us. It also has the ability to hear other people's beepers and find those we are supposed to meet.

Here's how that invisible beeper or heaven's net inside of us works:

In our daily life, we can pass by many people on the street. If you live in a city, you may walk past hundreds of people every day. Now, you may have some connection to a few of these people. You may have known them in a past life. You probably didn't know most of the people you pass.

If we can walk down the same street and pass by each other with no interaction and no feelings, no attraction or aversion to each other, we can say *the net is thin between us.*

But if we walk past and stop to notice each other, start to talk, get tangled up, then we say *that net is thick between us.*

For example, you might pass by dozens of beggars on the street, but for some reason, you stop and give one guy five dollars. Chances are, there is some net between you. Later, among thousands of people in the subway station, a pickpocket chooses you as his victim and sneaks up behind you to steal your wallet. The net between you and that thief is even thicker than between you and the beggar.

When we attract those who we have a thick history of net reactions with, trouble is possible, even likely.

That's why those old monks lived so simply, so gently, so humbly, so cautiously, and kindly. Their preference was to move through life unnoticed. They didn't want to disturb that net or draw attention to themselves because they didn't want to pull in those people with whom they shared lots of thick net.

If I'm in water and move very gently and slowly, I don't cause much of a ripple. I want to keep the water I move in as smooth as possible because when there is a ripple, other things can notice me. What I attract if I'm noticed are reactions from past actions. I risk attracting others whose net thickly entangles in some way with my own.

Those monks tried to move seamlessly, softly, interacting as subtly and kindly as possible with everyone and everything. They didn't want to "bump" haphazardly into that net and attract trouble.

You see, I'm no longer the same after I bump into that net. I start a reverberation as my thinking and actions affect others. It changes my life, my experience, for the entirety of my future. Then I bump into somebody else, and I'm changed again. It just keeps going and going, good or bad.

Likewise, those monks kept vigilant watch over their thoughts, endeavoring to keep their minds calm. They knew that nothing, not even our minds, can escape from this net.

They didn't want that net to even pick up a bad thought.

Can you make your mind not even move? That would be the best, but given that our mind is in constant motion and never stops, it is virtually impossible. That's why staying calm, keeping your thoughts positive, grateful, and hopeful, is the next best thing. That's why it's so important to know this principle. You need to understand there is a great incentive to learning how to manage your mind with DO science.

Let's say I'm often very angry, but I never say anything. I'm still vibrating that net with my anger. That anger travels along the net and hits a person connected to me but who I haven't met yet in this lifetime. It hits them because we have an angry past together. I may have even killed this person centuries ago out of anger. I didn't know that we were connected by that net because its action is invisible. Soon, she moves in next door. At first, I'm elated to have a new neighbor, but weeks later, we start to fight. Now we're connected, and I'm tangled up in a way that disturbs my peace and makes me miserable.

I didn't know about our past history and how I killed her hundreds of years ago. That neighbor is so angry at me, and she makes my life a living hell. But her anger is only a reaction to all the anger and trouble I caused her in a previous lifetime. If I hadn't been so angry in *this* life, she might never have picked up my signal on that web and been able to unconsciously find me and move in next door. My beeper sent out a signal that she picked up and recognized right away. The net was thick between us. Had I learned how to discipline my thoughts and quiet my anger, she might not have picked up my beeper's signal and found her way to my neighborhood.

How can one cope with this net? That's the main story of Eastern religion and philosophy. It's why they value yielding, why they try to relax, why they stay calm and receptive, why they advocate softness. It's not that they just wanted to be nice people or follow a moral code of conduct; they wanted to shut off their beepers.

What you also can't feel or see is that as you move through this net you are also traveling through many different overlapping dimensions. How many? It's hard to tell, but it could be:

TRILLIONS OF DIMENSIONS

As multidimensional beings, we are just like the Earth. Some people think of the Earth as a great big rock. But the Earth doesn't end at its physical boundary. It has an atmosphere. It has a magnetic field. It has a gravity field that's even further out.

We are like that. We have our physical body, and we also have our mind. We have our own energetic field made up of electrical pulses that also radiates through and around our body. We also have what many call our "spirit" and/or our "soul"—the invisible components that make us who we are.

Those old DO scientists knew that human beings had many different layers. They had different words to describe the many dimensions of ourselves. They called our life energy "Chi" or "Ki." They called our invisible spirit "Shen." They called our mind and its thinking "Yi," while separately calling our ability to think, that piece of DO inside us "Te."

We balk at the concept of invisible dimensions within ourselves or that we might have an invisible spirit that works outside of our normal conscious awareness. But are invisible dimensions so hard to understand?

There are purely physical dimensions of our own bodies we can't even see or feel. Can you feel your liver doing its job? Can you feel your immune system patrolling in your bloodstream? No. But just because they are imperceptible to our conscious mind doesn't mean they aren't critical to who we are and to keeping us alive.

In that way, your liver and your immune system are part of *you*, but in many ways, they exist in their own dimension beyond your awareness, even though you are intimately connected and one with them.

Let's go back to my house for more examples of how multiple dimensions interact. In my house, there are many living beings. Some I'm aware of, and some I am not. A mosquito has a mosquito's dimension. A fly has its own dimension; so does a cockroach. I might live and share the same physical dimension as they do, and it might look like we all share it in the same way, but we don't. A fly's eye is so different from mine—it might see a prism of 100 pictures when it lands on my sandwich. I have no idea what a cockroach thinks about or how it sees the world from under the kitchen baseboard.

Likewise, my world is just as mysterious to them as theirs is to me. Our human world is so gigantic and complex that a mosquito or fly can't really perceive it. Do mosquitos or flies have any conception of Wall Street or what a rocket ship is or who is president or where the bread on my sandwich comes from? I don't think the mosquito cares about the television show I'm watching or knows that it's different from the moon in the window. Our human world is outside of their dimension. Even though they are living right here with us, they can't perceive more than a small fraction of even the simplest physical part of our human world, much less all of its dimensions. They are limited by their mind and senses.

Now all of us can share this physical space while continuing to live in our own dimensions: the mosquito, the cockroach, the fly, and me. We're all in the same house, and everybody goes about their own business without conflict most of the time.

But once in a while, we have a skirmish. The mosquito bites me, and I slap at it. The cockroaches eat the poison my exterminator left in the corner. The fly leaves bad bacteria on my sandwich and the next day I feel sick. Our dimensions have now crossed each other, and we come into conflict. And at least to the mosquito and the cockroach, and maybe even me, that conflict can be deadly!

Our dimensions here on Earth collide together all the time. I can take a walk to the store and kill thousands of ants and microbes on the sidewalk without even realizing it. Our differences of size, form, intellect, and physiology block our awareness of each other, to the smaller dimension's peril. If those ants could see me coming or knew they built their sandhill on a sidewalk right next to the grocery store, they might be able to relocate and get out of the way. Unfortunately, I and the grocery store are out of their awareness because we are too large.

Extreme largeness can also hide one dimension from another. Those enormous galaxies out in space sometimes collide with each other. It looks violent, but if you lived on a planet inside one of those galaxies, you probably wouldn't even feel it because there is so much empty space inside each galaxy.

Although I live in a different dimension than a mosquito, I can still see him, and he in some way can still see me or at least sniff out my blood. At least we share the fact that we're physical beings. But dimensions aren't always material or substantial. Some dimensions are invisible.

Even human dimensions can be invisible. For example, each person on this planet has their own dimension. Each person's experiences and thoughts are different. That means that, in some way, each unique human being has an individual point of view and way of seeing and interacting with the world—their own individual dimension! So in one household, there may be a Walter dimension, a Susan dimension, and a Walter Jr. dimension.

We not only have our own individual dimension, but we also have many other shared dimensions. I live in the United States, so I share a dimension called "American" with millions of other people. We have a unique history, a certain culture, a particular style of government, and a specific set of laws that apply only to "Americans."

A doctor lives in her own dimension of medical science, terminology, and professional conduct. But when she gets home, she might also be part of another dimension called "mother" or "wife," and on Sundays, she is part of a dimension called "Catholic." As a man who is not a doctor and not a Catholic, I might think I know a little bit about these dimensions because I can observe them. But I've never been to those dimensions, and I never will because I can't. I'm stuck in my own set of dimensions for now.

Now here comes the tricky part: we as individuals have our own inerasable record of actions and interactions with heaven's net. Our record notes both the good deeds as well as the suffering and liability we've caused over time. That's called our individual karma.

But every other dimension, be it a mosquito's, a dog's, or shared collective dimensions like nations, religions, and professions, also are a part of and made from heaven's net. They all leave an inerasable record and suffer rebound reactions too! They can all have karma!

We as a species have our own collective human dimension. And guess what? We have a very bad credit report on that net. We've done immense damage as part of the collective action that we all share, and we have to pay that debt off!

So now you see that what we narrowly call "our dimension" is actually where trillions of dimensions all overlap each other. But they all come from Dimension One, and this one, DO, is there all the time in each and every one, carrying the record and consequences of our combined actions.

Yet we, in our arrogance, think that intelligence, life, meaning, purpose, and being can only exist here in "our dimension," and that, when we leave this dimension, it all disappears. That is a very limited point of view indeed!

These examples of other dimensions illustrate that invisible dimensions, for example, whatever invisible place those particles go to when they wink out of our physical world and come back again, or where the real part of Grandma goes when she dies, can also overlap ours.

Those are the invisible dimensions of our universe we can't see. But our piece of DO—that ability to think—

can see and understand, whether we consciously do or not.

And since those dimensions overlap with ours, they can affect what happens in our lives, just like I affect the lives of the mosquito in my house or the ants on my sidewalk.

That's why it's beneficial to know and be able to see what's going on in dimensions we cannot apprehend with our conventional five senses. Through DO, we can get out of the way if we see a hazard coming or see the truth about why another person is in our lives.

When we are cut off from our DO ability to think, we are no different than the ants on the sidewalk baffled by the foot traffic. We can't perceive the reason why and how such powerful forces are hurting us, and we can't know when to move out of the way.

DEFUSING KARMIC DYNAMITE

What the old religions called "sin" is more like a residue or tattoo left on that piece of the net that is "me." On an energy level, it functions like that "beeper" we talked about that pulls in people and events connected to your past actions.

Have you ever seen wildlife shows where they hunt and tranquilize a rare animal so they can staple a tag to its ear? That tag often has a chip inside that can be picked up by a remote sensor back at the park ranger station or even by satellites in space. They want to track that animal wherever it goes to study its behavior.

When I do something bad or hurtful, I'm like that animal that's been tagged. My sin starts to send out a signal.

Part Five: DO Science

Everyone involved in that hurtful deed can pick up that tag signal and find me—beep, beep, beep. Plus, my tag is clearly stamped that I am the original cause of the hurt.

Let's say I've just done a very bad thing; to me, it feels harmless. I haven't felt any consequences at all! It seems that I can go on living a very happy, successful life. I can even forget about the lady I insulted or the victim I cheated or the hit and run accident I fled because I haven't run into that part of the web that's started to send my consequences back to me. I haven't touched the part of the net with that record of that past—*at least not yet.*

However, because I have a tag that brands me as the cause of those negative actions, it's as if I'm walking around with a stick of dynamite in my pocket. I can carry that stick of dynamite around my entire life, and it might never explode. It never explodes because, for whatever reason, I've never walked near a fireplace or anything hot, and no one snuck up behind me and lit the fuse, so that fuse never ignited. That's why I have the false feeling of safety. I might even walk around for years with that stick of dynamite in my pocket and even forget about it!

The dynamite we all carry around is invisible. I may not even know or remember my bad deeds, so I don't even know that the dynamite is there.

Let's say you have a genetic predisposition toward alcoholism, but in this life, you are never exposed to alcohol. You never even saw anyone drink because you grew up in a religious home in a small town and lived there all your life. So that dynamite, invisible to you, never explodes. You conclude, "Ahhh, I'm such a good person compared to those people on television who drink and get in so much trouble!" But your pride is an illusion because you've never encountered the flame that would set your dynamite off.

One day, you leave that town and move to the big city. You get a fancy new job that requires a lifestyle where cocktails are an expected part of your social life. Boom! The fuse on your dynamite finally caught fire, and soon, your newfound lifestyle ruins your life.

Maybe someone had a past life of cheating people out of money in gambling games. In this life, he has that tag still attached. He is destined to lose a lot of money, over and over and over again. He's destined to become a gambling addict! But for whatever reason, he never goes near a casino and is never offered a chance to gamble or even learn how. He is okay because that outside factor never presents itself.

But what he can't see is that the net remembers his offense. The repercussions of his bad deeds are traveling toward him silently. One day, his company plans a conference in Las Vegas. When he goes to a casino, he's instantly mesmerized and loves it! The net inside and outside connects! Boom!

In order for karma to work, you need that outside net to connect with the inside net to set off the consequences. You can push a wheelbarrow full of bad karma, just like a wheelbarrow full of dynamite. But if you never introduce a factor to start a fuse on fire, it's as if that dynamite hibernates.

You can't trust that the karmic dynamite you carry will sleep forever. Ideally, you want to get rid of that dynamite before it explodes. But since you can't see it and don't even know it's there, you first have to have some way to identify that dynamite. Then you have to have the ability to get rid of it. You have to see the past repercussions that are problematic and following you around and somehow neutralize them *before* the consequences return.

Learning how to see past karma and resolve it can take many years of Taoist training. Before you have the ability to both identify and resolve it, you can stay safer thanks to DO science. You can protect that internal net from a wide range of possible triggers, even before you know whether or not they could hurt you. That's why there were so many precepts for those old monks about no sex, no alcohol, no money, no marriage, no conventional amusements. They knew those were common dynamite traps. They wanted to develop the ability to see and know through DO before risking stepping out too far on that web and setting off one of those traps.

If you can specifically identify what your weakness, past life "sin," and karma are before they are set off, you're in great shape. When you can do that, you don't have to be a hermit in a cave anymore or seclude yourself in a life of austerity like those old monks. You know you have dynamite, so you know that you can walk outside as long as you don't get close to anybody carrying a torch or a book of matches. Conversely, you also know that it's perfectly okay for you to go swimming because water won't light your fuse; in fact, it may even help you keep your dynamite under control and too hard to light!

In real-life terms, through DO ability, you might see that flying in airplanes could be dangerous for you, so you take a train or a ship when you travel. Or you might see that any drug could lead to addiction for you, so you're careful to only take medicine when you need it, never for recreation.

Even though they were great DO scientists, Buddha and Lao Tzu were also subject to this web. During Buddha's lifetime, one famine was so bad that he couldn't find any food. When he went begging, people gave him horse feed and corn cobs to eat. Buddha was able to touch DO and pinpoint the past encounter that caused him to have to suffer through that famine and explained it to his monks.

Jesus was able to see trouble coming in the garden of Gethsemane. He prayed to avoid it, but in the end, he saw the danger too late. The soldiers came to arrest him and haul him to prison.

Sometimes our dynamite is invisible, but other times, you carry dynamite because you treasure it, and you won't give it away. You don't even know that it's bad; in fact, you like it! You're proud of it! And that's what will attract those consequences to come back to you.

Let's say I'm a woman carrying an imprint of having been cruel to my past spouses. The result could be that any husband I attract I this lifetime will be cruel to me. If I knew that, I could choose to stay single and live a perfectly happy life.

But it's not always as simple as it seems. That imprint inside might give me a very strong desire to get married or keep drawing me to irresistible but dangerous men. Or my stubborn ego makes me so proud that I boast, "I'm only attracted to bad boys!" So I might even know I carry that dynamite but choose to go ahead and light it anyway out of desire or self-will.

That's why those DO scientists taught their students to reduce their desires, ego, pride, and sense of self. They taught monks not to be slaves to those influences. They knew that our desires, pride, and stubborn sense of self are precisely what can pull us toward a lighted torch! If you let go of those desires, that ego, that pride, you might be able to sneak right past any disaster. And if you do enough good deeds, the harmful person and bad consequences might move off in another direction entirely, narrowly missing you.

The person carrying the torch that's ready to fire up your dynamite doesn't always know they carry a torch either. A truck drives through a red light and runs into your car, causing your death or injury. The truck driver never intended to do that. Neither you nor they knew that you both carried a thick piece of tangled web with you that made the accident almost inevitable. You had accidentally killed him in another life. An invisible force pulled the two of you toward each other in this one.

Physicists call that gravity—two things pulling toward each other by an invisible force. There's another force that causes two objects to reject and move away from each other—the force of repulsion. They function like two sides of a magnet: magnets can either snap together by attraction or push and deflect each other through repulsion. These are the two forces of yin and yang, inward and outward, that we've explored at length before. But in DO, we see these same forces at work in our personal interactions and human affairs.

Sometimes you instantly "click" with another person. It's as if you've been friends forever. Wherever you go in your neighborhood, they pop up in the same grocery store, in the same park. That's the law of attraction at work.

If the net's invisible force causes two objects to repulse each other, you can never can put them together.

You probably will never even meet the people separated from you by repulsion power.

Attraction and repulsion also work on conditions and events. Some people make friends wherever they go or effortlessly make a profit no matter what business they invest in. For other people, no matter how hard they try, they can never get rich or make friends or have the sort of luck they see others enjoy. So that same web or chewing gum that causes you to stick in one place may prevent you from going to another. The same gum that pulls someone into you can pull them away.

This gravity and repulsion power applies to human thinking and human behavior in a way that unfolds according to a strict program. Together they form a pattern and create boundaries based on what each person's past actions allow for them in this lifetime.

How does this work? It's all conducted through the ability to think. The web of DO is the "governor" that regulates the forces of attraction and propulsion.

If you can think about something, that's because the web allows you to think it. And if you cannot think about something, it's because the web doesn't allow you to think about it, and your brain is blank.

If your piece of the net says you can never be wealthy, you'll never have the right idea at the right time when it comes to investing or starting a business. Conversely, you'll be susceptible to wrong ideas that lead you to lose or waste money.

Each person's internal web of past actions expresses itself in interests and ideas as well as aversions and blockages that steer them through life. This is why some people are interested in math, while others like music or

Part Five: DO Science

somebody else doesn't like music. If they are strong in one area of life, they are probably very poor in another area because of that web effect of attraction and repulsion.

Is this predestination? Yes and no. It's more like predetermined limits of how far you can go in any direction. As long as you stay within certain parameters, you have lots of choices. But the minute you try to go further than your chewing gum can stretch, it will snap you back into those limits to play out the course of what the net has already sent on its way to you.

If your program says you must drive from Chicago to Boston, you can take lots of different routes. You can take routes that are fast or slow, historic or scenic, on highways or backroads. You have many different choices on your drive to Boston. But if you turn your car around and start heading toward San Francisco instead, at some point, the road will be closed. There will be detours and maybe even a traffic cop in place to order you to turn around and head back toward Boston.

That's why in life, you can set goals and make choices. Sometimes heading toward those goals and choices is delightful, rewarding, and relatively easy, and sometimes you meet with obstacle after obstacle. The reason lies in how much resistance you are encountering in heaven's net or pushing the limits of what your program allows. Sometimes the current and waves push you where you want to go, and sometimes they make it very hard or even tip your boat over.

That's why DO science advises us to "flow." If we follow our program instead of fighting with it, we'll find life is much smoother. Like flowing with the river, we slow down and go with the current when waves are high. We wait for the stormy water to calm down before we try and paddle upstream. Meanwhile, we aren't just passive. We are actively learning and practicing our DO science to smooth our way.

MANAGING EMOTIONS

Insight into Dimension One not only helps us understand our thinking, but it can help us understand and better manage our emotions.

We worry and feel out of control when we experience rage, fear, sadness, or grief. Psychologists and life coaches offer us many theories and practices on how to calm our emotions, but we still seem to be overwhelmed by them more often than we'd like to be.

The key to managing emotions is to stop and consider: "What gives me that *ability to feel* anger, sadness, or fear? For that matter, what is the substance that allows me to feel love, excitement, and joy?" The substance that enables your ability to feel is the power of DO. Emotions are just like thoughts. They ride on top of that original ability.

You will find little success if you deal with thoughts and emotions at the level of thoughts and emotions. You will only be able to change them and master them if you can go to the source power they ride on. Meditate and focus on that underlying ability, and you can cut right through those negative thoughts and emotions and go to that original DO power those thoughts and feelings are stealing as fuel.

When we feel hate or fear, we need to stop and be grateful that we have the ability to hate. What gives us

Part Five: DO Science

that ability? If I truly become aware and grateful of that ability, see the miracle of its power, and see it as my connection to DO, then eventually, I realize that I no longer want to waste that ability on garbage like hate or fear.

I only have a limited amount of time here on this earth, and I wish to use it well. It's as if my body were a cell phone with limited battery life. If you were on a trip and your cell phone only had half an hour left on the battery, but you didn't have access to a cell phone charger, you'd take care to conserve that battery time. You'd carefully save it for an emergency or an important call, not use it to play video games.

We have 60–80 years of life, more or less. Are you going to use up that battery life on garbage?

But instead of carefully watching over your cell phone and its last precious minutes, your kids steal it to play games, burning up your last half hour. Then, when you suddenly really need to use that phone—oops—the time is all gone.

You have to look at your life this way. Wasteful, unproductive thoughts and emotions are a waste of that ability and battery life. Thoughts like fear, anger, revenge, and jealousy are like mischievous kids playing games on your battery time. That's why the Buddhists call emotions "thieves."

The same energy potential that gives you the ability to be angry can also give you the ability to be very happy, to express kindness to someone who needs it, or the ability to practice to recharge your battery. The power is yours to enjoy, save, or squander, depending on how you use it.

Once again, the key to controlling how you use your emotional energy is to shift your focus from the emotion back to the ability that is at its root. In fact, once you learn how to focus on your ability to feel rather than the feeling itself, you can turn your emotions around very easily and learn to stabilize yourself.

Once we identify the powerful ability that fuels our feelings, it's very tempting to want to use it to stay happy all the time. But guess what? Happiness, although far preferable to grief or anger, also burns up that battery time.

That's why Taoists, instead of chasing happiness, used their battery life to create more battery life! By finding a state of calmness, not spending too much on any strong emotions (either positive or negative), they were able to go deeper into their connection with DO and use practices like Taichi, Qigong, or Tao Gong to refuel themselves and charge back up. That's why you'll find historical records of Taoists living well over one hundred years.

We want to go beyond all emotion and think back to that ability to feel and think. If you say, "Anger is no good; I am going to stay happy all day," you have a problem. You still aren't centered on that root ability. It's like saying, "I'm not going to lean on that wall. I will lean on this other wall instead." Leaning on either wall is incorrect. You must stay centered and straight to connect to DO, not depending on even good emotions, but rather depending on that ability to feel, to think, to live.

In addition, whether you are happy or angry about a situation usually depends on a judgment you've made inside based on your thoughts and memories. Those thoughts and memories could be true or false. More often than not, they don't give a full picture of the situation. Most likely, your thoughts and memories are based on only partial truth. By going back to the original ability behind all feelings and thoughts, you not only calm down the emotion but get a better understanding of the whole big-picture truth of the situation at hand.

Whenever something makes us prideful, happy, worried, angry, we automatically detach from that DO ability and start burning up the limited fuel in our battery. Worse, I not only burn energy, but I can also load a bad program into my thinking. Perhaps I draw a wrong conclusion from my anger that colors my judgment for the rest of my life. Or I allow myself to get so angry that I carry a life-long resentment or prejudice. These "bad programs" in our thinking can block us from the pure mind we need to see the truth and connect back to DO. In that case, it's as if my internal computer has been hacked so badly that I need an antivirus program to get it running smoothly again.

What's a virus in your thinking? Here's the test: Whatever you cannot make a newborn baby do or think but you do or think anyway—that's a virus. You cannot say anything that can make a newborn baby angry, jealous, fearful, or excited. They are immune to that. Unless you shout or make silly faces while you talk, they'll just sit there sucking their fist, looking at you. You can tell them they're ugly or that you stole their trust fund. They won't care. You have to program a baby while it is growing up to react with the kind of complex feelings we allow ourselves to suffer from.

From the time you were a baby, you grew up assimilating all sorts of fake programs, like viruses, that tell you how you should think and feel. If someone calls you a bad name, you are programmed to become offended or mad. If you cry hard enough, you are programmed to think you might get candy, comfort, or a kind word to soothe you as your mother did. If you grow up in parts of Africa, you are programmed to think that fat people are fortunate, wealthy, and attractive. If you grow up in California, you might be programmed to think that fat people are gluttonous, unhealthy, or lazy. Both sets of judgments are just programs that may or may not be true in any given situation; therefore, they aren't really true or useful.

These viral programs divorce you from that pure mind you had as a baby. Because the programs are so unconscious and so woefully inadequate for most situations, as an adult, you find yourself confused, miserable, and ineffective. You then reach out to a fake self-help guru or fake religious dogma to rescue you from the fake virus. That guru or dogma gives you even more partial, manufactured solutions. Those manufactured solutions only add another layer of programming that trains you how to think and feel, ultimately making everything worse.

The solution is to get rid of all that fake thinking and fake feeling based on your fake programmed reactions to life. Learn how to meditate and get in touch with that pure ability again. Then you can more easily shake off those viruses on your own. You can react to each situation in the moment from pure awareness and spontaneous pure feeling from the true ability of DO inside you.

Ancient Taoist masters also practiced moving meditations such as Taichi, Qigong, and Tao Gong, not just to refuel their battery life but as tools to reprogram themselves back to pure mind and pure awareness. They serve as an antivirus program for your mind. That's part of how these practices helped them tap into the power of DO.

THE TRUTH ABOUT SUFFERING

People wonder why suffering and bad times seem to be a constant in our world. No matter what station they hold in life, it seems everyone has their share of suffering. Some people have a larger share of suffering, some a smaller share, but everyone feels pain over some aspect of their lives. Ultimately, we all experience illness, aging, and death.

Suffering is inevitable. Why? Once Neng creates something, that creation moves out and away from the stillness of DO and into action. Once Neng creates something, we already have Dimension Two. It is no longer pure Dimension One anymore. It is a downgraded version of itself and loses the full potential of DO.

In Dimension Two, Neng folds space upon space to create, compressing nothingness into something. As space folds upon space, it becomes material. The denser and tighter the folding, the less emptiness is there. Neng is still there but can't move that object as freely as it can move its own nothingness nature. Neng can travel through any space, even that space between the atoms and particles that make up a rock, but because it's pulling itself in tightly to create that rock in and of itself, it is now frozen and cannot move anymore. On a primary level, this is where "suffering" comes from.

A law of any dimension outside of DO is suffering. That's because any *dimension outside of DO is separated from its whole and ultimate truth.* This is why suffering never ends, no matter how high you go in your spiritual achievement. Wherever you are, high, low, solid, insubstantial, whatever dimension you're in, you are still separate from DO to some extent, and you suffer. The more you can tune back into DO, the more you can reduce and manage that suffering or make that suffering more productive.

"Why should one treat misfortune as part of his own body?
The reason I have misfortune is because I have a body.
If I do not treat my body as my own, why should I have any misfortune?"

Tao Te Ching, Chapter 13

Folded into a material body and getting trapped there is suffering. That's Neng. But unfolding ourselves in order to escape that trap is also suffering. That's Kong—trying to return to DO. When our body decays enough to finally release our spirit back on its journey to DO—we can often experience that as suffering! It's like ripping the bandage off.

Suffering is always part of the story, but it's not the whole story. Neng coming into being as a part of creation isn't only suffering; it is also joyous. We can see, feel, and experience beautiful and amazing things in a body and through our thinking, feeling, and senses. And even decay and death don't have to be suffering; they can also be joyous. We can finally be free of this body and experience the release from it.

Part Five: DO Science

Coming into being is suffering. Escaping being is suffering. Coming into being is joyous. Escaping being is joyous. Both Neng and Kong travel together everywhere they go. They are the two separate sides of the wholeness of DO. Depending on what state they're in, they can both bring either joy or suffering.

Suffering and pleasure alternate for everyone. Even if you see someone doing very well with no trace of suffering, it is just because they are going through the pleasant phase of that alternation. Sooner or later, they will go through a period of suffering too. The higher the enjoyment and pleasure phase, the bigger the crash or suffering phase. It's just another circular cycle. It is part of the inward and outward function of DO. There is nothing you can do about this.

Even those old Taoist masters weren't immune to suffering. However, they learned how to manage suffering through understanding DO. First of all, they understood it was just a cycle, that after a period of suffering, relief and joy were bound to return again.

They understood that they could even out that swing cycle of pleasure and suffering so that their highs and lows were very moderate. They led moderate, unprovocative lives. By not seeking extreme pleasure, they avoided extreme pain.

We can be like them by accepting what comes, staying calm, and being careful about what we initiate.

Let's say you are bored and think that you'd rather be happy. You go to a bar to relieve that suffering through alcohol and dancing. You may have a very good time. But the crash later is proportionately just as bad. You wake up with a hangover and perhaps many regrets. That hangover reminds you that happiness and suffering come together as a pair and are always alternating with each other.

The Taoist, on the other hand, would be more likely to learn how to accept the temporary and manageable suffering of an eventless evening rather than try to solve it by choosing intense happiness at a bar. The Taoist knows that intense happiness will be accompanied by intense suffering afterward.

Over time, through DO science, you can learn how to weather and flow with the challenges and suffering life deals out to you, creating a stable and resilient life rather than one with dramatic ups and downs. You can even learn to be content with calmness and peace rather than crave intense excitements—most of which never seem to satisfy us in the long run anyway.

Many self-help and spiritual teachers push us to strive continually for happiness. It's as if happiness is a barometer for spiritual achievement. We start to feel that if we are not happy one hundred percent of the time, we are failures. On the other side of the coin, certain religions or philosophies teach the opposite—that we should always be sad, fearful, and ashamed and seek to reduce any pleasure in our lives, and that only bad things wait in store for us in the future. This is also unbalanced.

If I only see the beautiful side of life, that's just half of the truth. If I only see the bad in life, that's also only half of the truth. If I take the opinion that everything in this life is and should be beautiful, the side effect is that everything will eventually become so ugly to me. Think of those who get high on opium or smoke pot or drink alcohol. They do so because, under that influence, everything is wonderful and beautiful. But when the effect wears off, the side effects are awful. In the throes of an addict's craving and withdrawal, everything appears to be and feels like hell.

The same is true of mental opium, such as practices exclusively devoted to pleasure and happiness. When we are trained to only accept happy people, happy events, and happy thoughts, eventually, the harshness of the real world can creep in and cut us deeply with its sharp contrast.

Instead of seeing the world as either happy and beautiful or horrifying and cruel, the Taoist sees the truth—that our world holds both good and bad, and everyone experiences a bit of each. If I can tolerate enough suffering in order to rise above this continual alternation of opposites with my eyes wide open, then I can see that both suffering and happiness arise together from the same source. You can never have one without the other.

"Under heaven all can see beauty,
for there is already ugliness.
All know there is good, for there is already evil.
Therefore, having and not having emerge together.
Difficult and easy lie opposite to each other.
Long and short compare;
high and low lean upon each other.
Voice and sound harmonize each other;
front and back follow each other.
Therefore, the saint exercises 'non-action' to do things..."

Tao Te Ching, Chapter 2

and

"Calamity forever alternates with prosperity"

Bodhidharma, *Outline of Practice*

To conquer the pain of our constant alternating between happiness and suffering, we have to turn our mind activity around and go back to the source of both happiness and suffering. What enables me to feel both suffering and happiness? What is the ability in me that can even notice the difference? What mechanism governs the unforeseen experiences that come my way? That source is where Dimension One is.

When we can take our mind off of happiness and suffering and recognize DO instead, we don't have to initiate any dramatic solutions to our suffering. We just allow the activity of DO to unfold in our lives, manage and accept what comes our way with calmness and assurance, and eventually, the ups and downs in our lives start to even out. We learn and accept that bad feelings are mostly transitory, as are good ones.

"Look! A gusty wind will not last all morning.
Showers can't last the whole day . . .
Rather, people who exercise the Tao should be
one with Tao."

Tao Te Ching, Chapter 23

This sounds easy to do, but it's not. It flies in the face of everything we know to be at the heart of human nature. It is human nature to avoid suffering and chase pleasure. To pursue Tao, you must defy everything in the human world. Everybody pursues happiness and avoids pain. They are like two walls we bounce between. Instead, we should try and stay in the center. Between happiness and pain is where the highest achievement and power is found. When you're immersed in happiness, you are off-center. When you have pain, you are off-center. The center is calm and neutral.

To maintain a connection to DO, we must learn to avoid both sides. If one side is brave, then one side is cowardly. Both are wrong. If one side is happy, then one side is sad. Both are wrong. If one side is beautiful, then one side is ugliness. Both are wrong.

Any and all such comparisons will blind you if you let them. Why? Because both sides arise from the same source DO. When you realize that, you can rise above the opposite and alternating states and connect to the truth. That's what we call staying in the center or "the middle way."

Any pair of opposites distracts us from DO, as DO is one piece, one power, one truth. We want to stay in that truth. That is why in our practice, we work toward the three Cs: Calm, Comfortable, Centered. When I have these three Cs, I'll be less likely to be driven by happiness or sadness because then I cannot feel and follow DO.

NO CONFLICT, NO ESCAPE

When you cultivate calmness and tiptoe on heaven's net, you don't try to fight the negativity in your life the same way. Instead of raging, complaining, or punching at our obstacles, we again try to stay in the center. Your aim is to deal with any conflict in a way that softens and harmonizes the situation.

In ancient Taoist "mouth-to-ear" teaching, they often talked about DO science as part of martial arts training. One rule in Taoist martial arts is dealing with an opponent this way: "No conflict, no escape." It's wise advice to apply in any situation when heaven's net sends you unpleasant consequences, enemies, and trouble.

The first part of the advice is "no conflict." We never want to push directly against our opponents. Instead, we want to move in harmony and skillfully steer him away, so we don't get hurt!

We need to learn to treat the obstacles in our lives the same way. Our life can be going along smoothly until we run into a sharp and hurtful event. It's like we've stepped on a nail sticking out of a board! If you get angry and smash your hand down on a board with the nail sticking up, you'll only hurt your hand. But if you approach that nail slowly and wiggle it from side to side, then maybe you can loosen that nail and pull it out. Then you can deal with that board in a more constructive way.

Similarly, if you thrash and vigorously try to get out of a sticky spider's web, no matter how hard you try to tear yourself out of it, you'll just get tangled up more. But if you move gently, softly, maybe you can peel off enough of the sticky stuff to keep going.

The other piece of this advice is "no escape." In martial arts, we never want to lose contact with our opponent. We stay connected to him so we can feel and sense where he is moving next so we can redirect his force or get out of the way.

The same is true of conflict in our lives. We never want to simply run away from a difficult situation when it's ours to face.

Part Five: DO Science

You see, once you learn the science of DO, you get very clear on one thing: if you throw a ball at this net, it bounces back at you with no exception, no escape. Nothing and no one are immune. Pretty soon, you try *not* to throw *any* balls at that net. You walk away and try to escape. But that's unwise in the long run.

It's easy to avoid people and situations that bother us. We can run away and never speak to our foes again. Many of those old monks tried that. They escaped to temples and caves to avoid the inevitable suffering of karma. But could they really escape? No. After all, in what cave in which mountain can you avoid aging, illness, and death?

Wiser DO scientists understood that meeting up with trouble caused by our past presents an opportunity to resolve it. After all, it's not going away on its own. If we run, it will still find and chase us forever—even in our future lifetimes. If we deal with it the right way, we won't have to meet it again and again down the road.

These wise monks saw the goal of DO science as learning to softly meet, welcome, and skillfully manage trouble. In practicing these abilities, the Taoist learns to "flow." They can sense what is coming in the net and harmonize with it, cooperate with it better, so there are less damage and less risk of conflict. They can reduce its momentum so that the next time that particular wave hits them, it isn't as strong.

When you were a kid and learned how to play catch with a ball, you quickly learned that a fast-moving baseball or football hurts your hands. It especially hurts if your hands are outstretched and stiff when you're trying to catch it. You end up in conflict with the ball's momentum and usually end up losing the ball as it bounces off your hands.

You eventually learn that if you see the ball coming, you can avoid the hurt by either (1) getting out of the way or (2) receiving the ball gently with your entire body curving and absorbing the shock of the impact.

If you choose number one and just keep running out of the way when the ball comes, you'll never learn how to be a good ballplayer. Good ballplayers learn how to "neutralize" the force of the ball, using their entire body to catch the ball. Learning how to catch properly reduces any sting or injury.

The same is true for "catching" incoming suffering or trouble sent by heaven's net as a rebound of your past actions. You can soften your reception to adversity. You can learn to greet the down times productively instead of feeling in conflict with them. You can turn them into productive learning time, cultivating good deeds and gratitude despite the hardships. That will build a better future than complaining or fighting or running away.

In those martial arts talks, we talk about practicing as often as possible in order to "sharpen your knife." In martial arts, we mean practicing our self-defense skills. But it's also the DO science of learning how to deal with life challenges.

If you want a good knife, you have to know how to sharpen it. To do that, you need a stone. We can look at each challenge our karma throws at us as a whetstone to sharpen our knife. If we simply hit our knife edge against the stone, we can damage and dull our blade. If we constantly confront unpleasant people by fighting with them, it's like hitting our blade against the stone.

If we refuse to bring our blade to the stone, soon that knife will grow useless and dull and will sit in the corner and rust. That's like when we run away and hide from the situations and people that bother us and never really resolve our problems or grow as a person.

But, if we use that stone instead to gently pass our blade across it at just the slightest angle over and over and over, we'll sharpen our blade. This means we can meet adversity calmly, looking for ways to stay in harmony with other people—neither running away from them nor engaging in conflicts.

Lao Tzu gives us an example of how it looks when we can successfully master "no conflict, no escape:"

"Deal with others with gentleness and kindness.
Speak with truth, governing everything well.
Ever capable, always act with right timing.
Only when there is no need for conflict,
then there is no fault."

Tao Te Ching, Chapter 8

Mastering "no conflict, no escape" not only neutralizes the assaults coming at us, but it prevents us from creating new bad deeds or new enemies.

You see, that rebounding net allows all things to "get even." If you want to calm that effect, you, too, need to give up any need to get even. If you don't, a record of your resentment will still remain in that net and pull you back into conflict with that same person or people. That's why smooth interactions and forgiveness are important.

*"After resolving a bitter quarrel,
some resentment is bound to remain.
How can this be considered good?
Therefore, a Taoist master keeps his loan receipt but does not push for repayment."*

Tao Te Ching, Chapter 79

and

*"Do not judge and you will not be judged.
Do not condemn and you will not be condemned.
Forgive, and you will be forgiven."*

Jesus, from Luke Chapter 6, Verse 37

If this was all visible, it would be a piece of cake. But often, the grindstones that are tossed at us are invisible, and we can't see them coming. If we can see and touch something, that means we can handle it, cope with it. But in this world, we are often blind.

Right this very second, you are moving through that net. In fact, the whole room you are in is moving through that net without you being even slightly aware of it. It's invisible and, in that way, deceptive! Since you can't feel or sense it, outwardly, that travel through this net seems smooth. It's smooth enough right now that you can sit and read. But what you don't know is what or who is already on its way to you tomorrow. Whatever unavoidable trouble or irritation lands on your doorstep, be sure to see it as a whetstone and practice no conflict, no escape.

YOU ARE YOUR OWN DOJO

Lao Tzu advises us to hold onto ancient origin when we deal with today. What he's saying is to not forget we are made of DO—because DO is our ancient origin.

Do we simply learn about Dimension One as an idea? No, it is more than an idea; we are right in it. We are made of it. So to apply the power of DO to our lives isn't about learning something new but rather discovering what we already have. DO is our origin, the fundamental source of our life, consciousness, and even our physical structure and beingness in this material world. We don't have to get it; we've got it.

When we were very young children and asked Mommy and Daddy, "Where did I come from?" they would say: "The stork brought you and dropped you down the chimney," or "We picked you out of a cabbage patch." They made up those stories and stopped their explanation right there because we weren't ready to hear the whole truth about human reproduction.

Later, perhaps when we were pre-teens, someone finally explained the facts of life to us. But even when we could understand the nitty-gritty of sexual intercourse, it only provided a partial explanation. Most of us, even today, still aren't able to answer the questions, "What comes before the sperm and egg? What gives them life and gives our children life and the ability to reproduce generation after generation?"

We cannot understand what comes before reproduction and what provides the spark of life because, like those very young children, we're not ready to receive the truth yet. In understanding the truth of life energy, we human beings are still in the stork and cabbage patch level of understanding. The real truth behind what makes us alive is endless because it goes all the way back to that DO.

To think that we are ultimately created by DO is hard for us because it's infinite. We as human beings can only think in finite terms, so we prefer explanations that include a beginning and an ending. We want a creator and creation, a subject and an object. We want everything to have a birth and death as we observe in our human lives. We can only think in terms of separation and boundaries.

DO has no beginning and no end; it's just there. You're not all of it, but you are a part of it and can never get out of it. That's why our minds cannot handle that we are made of this, created from this and that the origin of sperm and egg go all the way back to such potent and infinite nothingness. We'd prefer to think we came from a cabbage patch. It's more comfortable that way.

So we study biology, embryology and bring all our intelligence and learning to bear upon this cabbage patch way of looking at life and still cannot understand the most fundamental thing of all: Why are we alive? What gives us consciousness and the ability to think? We can "learn" all we want for the duration of time and still not find the answer because we are made of the answer and are using that answer to study the question of life itself. We are riding that cow and not even counting it.

Just like DO is the origin of our ability to think, DO is also the origin of life.

The way to know life is not to learn about it but to reconnect with our own energy of life: to feel, to flow, to experience it in a palpable, subjective, and direct way—

not an abstract philosophical one. We need to be one with DO, not just read about it.

This is why the Taoists of old created meditations like Taichi, Chi Gong, and Tao Gong—moving meditations that put living in motion, the feeling and flowing of life energy and meditation together. They discovered it to be the fastest way to make a connection with their own life energy and, by default—to their own DO inside of them.

I teach Taichi to all my students and have written many books on the subject. It is perhaps the fastest, most reliable way to experience the life energy we all carry inside. It also trains us to pay less attention to our thinking and more attention to our ability to think by focusing that ability on our true feeling, on our movement, on our life energy. When we join our ability to think with our ability to live, amazing things happen. It's like a shortcut to connecting with DO.

Taichi was actually passed down by martial artists, and many study Taichi as a martial art. But martial arts skill is not the real goal of Taichi. Touching DO is the real goal.

The most important martial art we need to learn is how to defend ourselves from our own thinking and our own ignorance about who and what we are in respect to the universe.

Do you know the term for where martial artists go to learn and practice? They go to their "dojo." It's pronounced dough-joe. The literal meaning of the word dojo in Japanese is "the place of the way." When you go to a karate dojo, you are going to a place to study the way of karate. If you go to an Aikido dojo, you are going to a place to study the way of Aikido.

But if you look at the original characters that make up the word dojo,

道 場 = Do Jo

the first character is the same character for the word Tao or "DO" that we are using for Dimension One.

Instead of going to a school, temple, church, or the library to study the Way or DO science, the best place of all to study DO is inside your very own being. You are your own dojo because you are a "place of the way" just as much as any other place on Earth. You are a direct contact point of DO with its life and ability to think, forming the very you of you. Your opponent in this dojo, your sparring partner, is your delusion that you are separate, your preference for artificial and limited thinking. The only person separating you from your infinite potential is you. The dojo where you learn to defeat yourself is you.

Jesus and his followers liked to talk about our bodies as temples. That is also true. But sometimes, before you can see and experience yourself as a temple, you first have to see yourself as a dojo.

In this dojo, there is no wrestling match with other people like other martial arts dojos. Here, you use the martial art of DO science to dissolve wrong ways of thinking that separate you from access to your DO potential. You use DO science to neutralize the incoming blows and kicks of karma. You use your DO martial art to throw away the forces that drive conflict and instead master harmony.

"Overcome others and you possess true force.
To master the self, develops true strength."

Tao Te Ching, Chapter 33

THE GOAL OF THE ORIGINAL TAOISTS

Those old DO scientists observed quite a bit about the way DO worked. But they didn't just research DO by watching it in action; they learned through actual experimentation and personal experience. Their own minds and life energy were their laboratories.

Their objective was to bring their awareness as close to DO as possible. To do this, they worked to drill down through everything that coated and covered up their original ability to think.

Our ability to think is already limited in that we're in a physical body. But we are also further limited by our thinking. Here is a diagram of what our thinking looks like. It surrounds and is fueled by our ability to think, but it also coats our ability to think like insulation.

Because my thinking serves as insulation, that means my ability to think is occupied by nonsense: dreams, rage, excitement, desire, longing, logic, and artificial intelligence. I'm too distracted to turn inside and realize there's an ability that provides me the means to do that. If I can use a method to tone down the activity of my thinking, my desire, my jealousy, etc., I can get calm enough to realize that I have some form of energy inside that gives me that ability to think and feel in all those different ways.

How can we chisel through all that insulation and get down to that ability to think? We need a very sharp tool. Ironically, we have to use our own mind as that tool. Thinking is troublesome, but there's an unfortunate fact we must face: Without this troublemaker, we cannot learn the truth. We must use that broken, rusty tool called thinking to dig down into that pure mind—our ability to think.

Why do we want to reach and connect with our ability to think? Let's abbreviate ability to think and call it "ATT." It's a great acronym because here in the USA, the biggest telephone company is American Telephone and Telegraph. We call it AT&T for short.

Why is AT&T the biggest telephone and communications company in the USA? Because they control the biggest network of cables and towers that can link you, no matter where you are, to anybody anywhere—as long as you can tap into that network. When you connect with AT&T, you can send and receive signals virtually anywhere on Earth.

Likewise, when we tap into our own ATT *(ability to think)*, we've tapped into the ultimate network that connects everyone, everywhere—the network of DO. DO is just like the phone company's fiber-optic and cellular tower network. It's continually sending messages to and from millions of people every second. To access this information, we must touch that cable or patch ourselves into that cellular network with our cell phone.

DO science will help you discover that our human body is designed to be a cell phone. It's designed so that we can plug into that network of DO. All of Taoist teaching and training had the aim of restoring our cell phone capability so we could patch ourselves back into DO via ATT—our ability to think.

When Alexander Graham Bell invented the very first telephone, he had a theory that we could "talk with electricity" by sending a wave of energy over a wire. A gadget he envisioned, called a "telephone," would then decode that energy wave into a message.

Bell's first telephone message was to his assistant in another room: "Mr. Watson, come here. I want you." Now Mr. Watson was probably amazed and elated to finally hear that faint and scratchy voice, but both men knew when he heard that, they had done it!

But then came the hard part. They had to figure out how to describe and demonstrate to others how it was possible for a message to travel over vast distances and come out of a dead piece of physical equipment far away from the original source. Otherwise, those who couldn't understand how this "telephone" worked might be scared and think it was witchcraft!

Lao Tzu had the same problem as Alexander Graham Bell and Mr. Watson. You see, he succeeded in tapping into this network of DO with his own "cell phone."

Here's how he described it:

*"It seems elusive and subtle, and yet within it is an image.
It seems subtle and elusive, yet within it is a form.
It appears vague and subtle, and yet within it is an essence.
This essence is very real, and therein lays a message."*

Tao Te Ching, Chapter 21

Okay, so he told us he did it! That he touched DO, that dimension of nothingness, and got a message. That means there is information there. That means it must be intelligent. But how did he do it? What equipment did he use? He goes on and tries to tell us more about that network and what it's made of and how he tapped into it—that it's eternal and made of our ability to think!

*"From the very beginning, until now its name has never been erased.
Thus, I can see and perceive everything within creation.
How do I know everything within creation?
Because of <u>this</u>."*

Tao Te Ching, Chapter 21

Ideally, you want your thinking to be not only fueled by DO but for DO to drive your thinking. If you use DO to do your thinking for you, you are automatically part of that network. It can both receive and deliver messages to any receiver in the universe. It can deliver information, pictures, sounds, anything you need.

If you subscribe to the services that AT&T provides, you can learn and know anything and visit anywhere or talk to any person, right from the comfort of your own home. You can find out the news in any part of the world, learn a language, study history, watch an opera, or conquer another world in a video game. That's because, in addition to phone service, AT&T offers television and internet too.

That's what Lao Tzu discovered about DO, too, by contacting his own ATT (ability to think). Without leaving the house, he could know and see everything!

"Never going outdoors,
yet he knows everything under heaven.
Never looking outside of the window,
he can see the Tao of heaven.
He who tries to act, the farther he searches,
the less he knows.
A Taoist master takes no action to investigate,
yet knows everything."

Tao Te Ching, Chapter 47

When you connect to that DO network, you can instantly pick up any information related to you. If someone is thinking about you, talking about you, or relating to you through forgotten history, you'll know. That network sends any messages related to you right to your "cell phone." Just like the phone company AT&T can trace your unique cell phone signal and track you wherever you go, that's true of the DO network too. And just like AT&T can keep a record of all your emails, transactions, phone calls, and contacts, so can DO—in the inerasable record of your thoughts and actions logged on heaven's net. It knows where to send "the bill."

How can we pierce down through all the layers of insulation and reach our own ATT inside? Through direct thinking. Direct thinking is called sincerity. True sincerity actually means no thinking. No-thinking is DO. If you are thinking, then you are already in Dimension Two, Dimension Three, Dimension 10,000, etc.

Lao Tzu describes direct thinking and sincerity like this: *"Can you be like a baby?"*

Using our pure mind and regaining that ability means dropping the numbness and mental limitations we've placed upon ourselves.

The first thing we need to do to restore our connection to DO is to remove routine thought. That's one reason moving meditation is such a big part of Taoist training—whether it be Taichi, Qigong, or Tao Gong. These are all moving meditations. Through moving meditation, we train our minds to focus on something other than our thinking. If I'm focused on the feeling of my breathing or the feeling of my elbow as it moves, I'm using that ability to feel, not think. It's like a trick! We trick ourselves because "feeling" with our mind is more pure, true, and sincere than "thinking." We are using our mind in a way that's closer to our own ATT and in a way that shuts off our artificial thinking.

We don't try to shut down our mind and its thinking. Our mind is like a monkey. It's that monkey's nature to jump and climb around and chatter all day. If we try to stop it, we can't. Instead, we give that monkey something to do—feel! First, we feel our breathing, then feel our body, and later, when we get good at feeling while we move, we can start to feel our life energy, which is closer to DO than either feeling or thinking.

That's the real goal of meditation. If we just sit there on a mat and let our minds wander, our thoughts will just go on and on, chasing one idea after another.

We are encouraged to chase ideas all our lives. We think thinking and learning are what will get us to our spiritual goal. That becomes a problem now because when I ask you to stop your ideas for even one minute, you have a very hard time doing so.

This is why Lao Tzu says, "Don't compete to be smart; if you get rid of all that, you'll actually know *more* through DO."

I don't want to be smart; I want that energy to enable me to be smart.

"Shut your knowledge, close the door of your cleverness, and life is ever full.
Open your knowledge, be busy with all your knowledge, and life is beyond hope of salvaging . . .
Instead, employ your inner light and return to insight."

Tao Te Ching, Chapter 52

Lao Tzu is trying to say: "Don't use your damn mind to think; use that original ability that enables you to do so in the first place!"

As we practice and grow more sensitive to our original mind, we find ourselves making new choices, responding differently, feeling differently about many situations. We "learn" organically inside, we feel right or wrong about situations, and our intuition and "hunches" become astoundingly accurate.

As that connection grows, you won't need books or conventional human knowledge anymore. You'll tap into a perpetual and infinite source of wisdom that can answer any question, address any problem, and guide you through life.

I sometimes jokingly advise my students to go home and throw away all their books. I say it in a really firm voice. They gasp in horror. (I know they won't throw them away. I have many books, too, that I enjoy.)

Did you ever read a great book, one that was so good, you were sad when you came to the end? You wished that book could go on forever, didn't you?

This book in and of itself is just a book. Keep it or throw it away. It doesn't matter.

But what matters is if you can grasp what's inside of it and make your own connection to DO through your ability to think. If you can even point yourself in that direction, you will open up a real and true adventure story, one that's uniquely your own that will go on forever.

Once you have that dynamic and real connection inside and can tap into that wisdom, then you can throw this book away like a piece of chewing gum stuck to your shoe.

Watch out, though! Everything you learned by reading here might stretch and follow you wherever you go.

CONCLUSION

Hopefully, this book has changed your view of both "something" and "nothing" forever. You'll never look at something the same way again because when you do, you'll see nothing. And you won't be working so hard to try and become something, but rather you'll be looking harder for that part inside of you that's nothing.

Now someone who hadn't read this book would be confused by what you just read above. But not you—you're no longer confused. You now know that nothing is the very first dimension, that nothing makes up all matter, energy, thought, time, and space. You understand it's Dimension One, the primary building block of all other dimensions, and that all of them follow the laws of DO.

You also know that the universal laws of Dimension One include the power to both pull inward and push outward, that it's round, invisible, inescapable, and most important of all, that it has and is the ability to think. You understand that nothingness responds according to Newton's Law of physics—assuring that every action, both tangible and intangible, has an equal and opposite reaction.

You are starting to think like a Taoist master when you now see how an understanding of Tao or DO applies simultaneously to science, psychology, religion, sociology, history, and philosophy.

Normally, a disciple in one of those ancient Taoist temples would need a decade or two to come to the same understanding you have if you've read this book carefully. That's because we have such a broader range of human knowledge to pull from than they did before. We can make so many analogies now that those old Taoist teachers couldn't. We can use gadgets like soccer nets, desk toys, and cell phones to describe how DO works. We can add those analogies to ancient ones that compared DO to emptiness, water, or an uncarved piece of wood.

A book that says everything, including you and I, comes from nothing and will return to nothing could be considered a downer. However, if you've been paying attention, you'll see that this is one of the most exciting, uplifting, hopeful, and encouraging messages of all time.

It would be fantastic if just by reading this book, you could understand enough to touch that DO inside of you and access heaven's net. You'd be able to instantly access the root of all intelligence, go beyond space and time, and be like those old Taoist masters.

But unfortunately, you can't become a Taoist master through reading books—no matter how many, no matter how detailed, no matter how old and authentic those books are—it's impossible.

Why? Because reading books only reaches that level of our mind we call "thinking." That's why in the oldest of Taoist traditions, none of the real teaching was ever written down. They didn't want you to get stuck in mere thinking.

They didn't write anything down partly because so many of them were illiterate. They also didn't write their

Part Five: DO Science

teaching down because they knew that the minute something is written down, it becomes dead and frozen in time. The message becomes trapped in the realm of the reader's thinking, and then it's vulnerable to misinterpretation, judgment, and false definitions. After all, Tao is "Bu Xiao," meaning "nothing like it." Any attempt to describe it with words will always fall short.

Instead, the way Masters taught disciples to connect back to DO was always through "mouth-to-ear" teaching. They called it "mouth to ear, heart to heart."

By spending time together, a student could ask their master questions, and the master could catch any wrong thinking or misinterpretation and offer a wide variety of analogies to help the student get and stay on the right track. They could dig down to the very bottom of any issue together. No topic was taboo.

After answering a key question about DO, a few days or weeks later, the master might ask that student to repeat what they learned. That way, the master could judge whether the student absorbed the answer and hung onto it intact or distorted it, or even forgot it altogether.

Actually, none of the best DO scientists ever wrote a book. Jesus never wrote a book. Buddha never wrote a book. Lao Tzu never wrote a book either. All of these ancient DO masters simply spent time in dialogue with their students and disciples. Most or all of the books written about what Jesus or Buddha said were written down by others much later after they died.

In Taoism, there was only *one* book that was dictated by and written down while Lao Tzu was still alive—the *Tao Te Ching*. We don't think Lao Tzu wrote it, but that it was transcribed by contemporaries of his who asked him questions and wrote down his answers. Every other book in Taoism is really a spin-off, an interpretation, an off-shoot of that first book, the *Tao Te Ching*. I like to joke with my students and say that every "Taoist book" written after the *Tao Te Ching*—including this one—is just "disinformation." Why? Because the translations or commentaries that followed would always be just off the mark of whatever Lao Tzu was saying "mouth to ear" in the precise moment to whoever it was that carved his words into those old slats of bamboo.

Just like after Jesus or Buddha died, after Lao Tzu died, his disciples and students enthusiastically tried to recapture his teaching in words and wrote many books. All of these Taoist books together sum up what scholars like to call "Taoist Thought." However, this makes no sense at all. It is the ultimate non sequitur. Why? Because ultimately, what makes a Taoist a Taoist is that a Taoist throws away "Taoist thought" and, indeed, all conventional thinking in order to reach their "ability to think." "Taoist thought" becomes just another layer of insulation between us and DO that we have to chisel through.

People often turn to "Taoist thought" to understand spiritual matters. They want to know about various gods, immortals, angels, and evil, life, and death. You can go ahead and study those fascinating religious and spiritual matters for decades, but you will still be at the mercy of those invisible forces until you give up "Taoist thought" and instead connect and use DO to understand them directly.

After all, where is evil? Where are angels? Where are gods or the devil? They are made of the same emptiness we are. They, too, are subject to the laws of DO.

When you connect with DO, you not only understand these matters, but you can navigate through them gracefully and productively rather than fall victim to the ups and downs of life in ignorance, despair, and counterproductive ways of thinking and living.

Other traditions call Dimension One "the Source," or Mother, Father, Creator, or Great Spirit. Whatever name or term, it points to a grand ultimate power that is above all else. In this book, we are calling it Dimension One.

You don't have to worship DO. Whether you worship it or not, its ultimate truths will operate the exact same way in your life and the world around you. Yet if you learn more about it, respect its laws, and apply those laws to your life, amazing things can happen. Whatever name you want to call it, or in whatever church you go to or don't go to, the ultimate truth applies in all situations, in all contexts.

Yet while you don't have to worship DO, it is very dangerous to worship anything *else* in any other dimension. Why? Anything other than DO is just a partial truth, a stepped-down version of reality, an attempt to separate or carve something off that uncarvable block. Whenever we try to split something off of DO and worship it, disaster normally follows.

Let's look at two of the things our human civilization has worshipped the most over time—gold and power.

What happens when we worship gold? The history of gold is blood-stained and tragic, but it is blood-stained and tragic precisely because so many people worship it. Everyone wants it. More people worship gold than worship the Pope or Dalai Lama because the notion behind gold is so simple: If I have more gold, I can do more things and have more things. We even believe gold can bring us intangible benefits like love, happiness, and respect.

But when you are murdered for your gold, robbed of your gold, create slaves to mine your gold in a state of suffering, build huge edifices to protect and house your gold, or your gold loses its value in the ups and downs of the market, you soon realize that gold carries much bloodshed, heartbreak, and burden along with it.

Another target of human worship is power or rulership. In the old days, people worshipped the emperor or king, thinking him to be divinely blessed as the son of heaven. Being king is so desirable because there is only one. The king is worshipped, obeyed, and has access to enormous wealth and privileges. But all that worship and love for a king can quickly turn to hatred. A king has to fight to protect his kingdom and also to maintain his position since others are willing to kill him and his subjects to take it. Being king can involve no small amount of bloodshed.

Kingship and gold are shiny and glamorous, but both have a very dark side to them.

Money, sex, reputation, beauty, all the lower-level things we worship, come with the same baggage. Everybody wants them, and because of that desire and worship, ruthless competition, bad feelings, and heartache are intertwined with all of them. If you don't have them, if you still worship them, and/or those around you all worship them, then the lack of them causes you to suffer or feel worthless and ruins your quality of life.

The more people desire something, the more likelihood there is for tragedy. It's inevitable. When people start to worship something other than pure ultimate truth, this is where the evil starts. And if you possess what everyone worships and wants—you are automatically cursed.

That's why it is better never to worship anything at all unless it is the original ultimate one power of DO that is the backbone of the entire universe.

To be able to feel and connect to DO, we need to get rid of every other dimension or partial truth about ourselves. That means we need to dethrone everything we unknowingly worship—our name, our Social Security number, our language, our law, our thinking, our gold, our king, our reputation. These artificial constructs created by our human society clog up our thinking. They separate us from our original potential and lock us into a limited dimension. Our mind is so dazzled and occupied by these thoughts, we forget about the miraculous power we possess in our inherent ability to think. When we aim so much of our attention at anything less than DO, we will fall short of our true potential.

We mistake a lot of temporary events for what is eternal; after all, gold can last a long time. If you think you "own" gold, even your idea of ownership is fake. Then when everybody fights over the ownership of gold, the reasons behind those fights are also fake. Fake always leads to more fake. When one fake thing leads to another and another, pretty soon, you cannot see the truth. One illusion leads to another among human beings. We accept them and pass them on to our kids and others; then, the illusions become more like a contagion. Those contagious ideas spread so far and wide until we are living a reality that's no more real than a movie.

When we devote ourselves to these small human fake ideas, respect them so much, put them ahead of our pure mind and pure connection to our life energy, they become like gods to us. Anything that dominates our attention and desire or limits our thinking and possibilities are things we unconsciously worship. We worship them because we give them credence over the ultimate truth. When we get rid of all these false ideas that we've worshipped in our minds for so long, it leaves us in a purer state of mind that allows us to touch our own ability to think.

That ability to think is the part of us that forms a bridge back to our full original potential. It is our connection to DO—pure unadulterated life energy and pure mind. This is the bridge the original Taoists were trying to build through their practice, simplicity, and rejection of outside influences in favor of the search for something more real, lasting, and eternal. They weren't trying to set up yet another set of ideas or cathedral of beliefs to worship—they were trying to tear down every partial truth, every false god, every distraction and return to clear, pure mind.

If we are to clear our minds and stop worshipping partial truth, where does that leave religion?

Even though worship is problematic when we aim it in the wrong direction, we shouldn't throw the baby out with the bathwater by condemning religion. Religious training is often very valuable. Why? Because it can be used as a tool that can help clear our mind.

As we've learned, so many religious laws and practices in all belief systems started as good advice to learn how to discipline ourselves and purify ourselves from worshiping wrong ideas. They were signposts pointing the way back to DO. For example, advice like, "Thou shall not kill, thou shalt not steal, thou shalt not envy anyone," tells you how to scrape away those false ideas you worship in your mind.

Religions told us not to "sin." But instead of viewing sin from simply a moral lens, we can now understand that false thinking, like envy, anger, fear, and greed, takes you further away from that pure ability to think. They unplug you from DO.

Without training and practice, you cannot shut all that down. You need to be able to shut those types of thoughts down to feel your pure ability to think. The training in many religions can help you do that if you can see and use their tools as an aid on your way to getting back to DO.

That's why the more you learn about Dimension One, the more you will understand what those old religious books were trying to say. Like every other form of human learning, we often misinterpret those old religious scriptures with our own prejudice and ideas until they lose their truth and become lists of "shoulds" and "should nots."

Most of those old religious figures like Moses, Buddha, Jesus, and others had made that connection deep inside themselves to the core of their life energy and mind, the DO inside of them. In turn, they did what they could to bring that truth to others. They used different words, different concepts like God, Father, Mind, or other names, but they all pointed back to the same universal One Power that governs everything everywhere.

That's why we hear stories of Moses, Buddha, Jesus, and those old Taoist immortals demonstrating their ability to perform miracles. What we saw as miracles, they experienced as the natural result of tapping into the full potential of DO.

There is no such thing as a miracle, only aspects of reality we do not yet understand. If you were able to travel several hundred years back in time and show somebody an X-ray of your hand and all its bones and tendons, they would consider that a miracle. If you told them it wasn't a miracle and tried to explain to them how an X-ray worked, they would laugh at you and think you were silly. The notion of invisible energy that could pass through skin and bones to take a picture would seem absurd, and if so, still a miracle.

Likewise, if a master or saint understands how to tap into Dimension One, it is possible that he or she can seem to do and see and know things that seem magical or miraculous. Yet, that master's miracles come from an understanding of how to connect to that ancient origin that is everywhere, knows everything, created everything, and is the source of all life, intelligence, and power. It's not the master or saint performing the miracles; it's their connection to DO in action and DO doing the miracles.

DO is so unique and all-powerful, yet so invisible, it's almost impossible to describe. That's why Lao Tzu used the word "Bu Xiao" when he referred to DO—"nothing like it."

If an ancient master or saint tried to explain DO to the common man, she would sound absurd and be at a loss for words to describe it. She would have to use analogies, parables, stories, or symbols to try and describe the indescribable. That's why so many truths handed down through the ages by those we call masters, avatars, or saints are misunderstood or considered too mysterious to understand. They were trying to describe Bu Xiao.

This book tries to describe Bu Xiao, too. We used dozens of analogies from spider webs to chewing gum and steel silos. Jesus used yeast, a mustard seed, and a pearl of great price. Lao Tzu used water, emptiness, and a block of wood. A hundred years from now, someone might pick up this book and start a new religion based on our own curious parables. But not one of our analogies can truly describe DO. DO is always Bu Xiao. There's nothing like it.

The more you understand DO, the clearer those old wisdom traditions and religions become. Also, the clearer their misinterpretations will stand out to you as well. The more you learn about DO, the more you may find yourself digging out those old holy scriptures from various religions to read them for yourself and reconsider what they might really be saying. There is hard DO science in most of those scriptures, but it hides underneath the surface dogma—under whatever insulation or secret code that evolved over time in that particular religion or culture.

When we go back and read those old classics and scriptures with a purer mind—a mind closer to DO, we have an almost instant understanding of them. This is because the more we practice, the more we are relying on the root power of our "ability to know" versus filtering what we read through previous man-made knowledge learned from other books, interpreters, and scholars.

But the best scripture, the best learning tool, is daily life. You might start to notice DO in your own life. You'll see how that Gong works for you as it sends back whatever you give it, or see how your own thoughts can isolate you in your own little dimension, or see the intelligent design that permeates our natural world.

And the next time someone tries to cut you off in traffic, you might just slow down and let them. You might be just a bit kinder to the cranky grocery clerk or think twice before sending that angry letter to your landlord. But it won't be because you're moral; it will be because you are a budding DO scientist who knows better than to disturb heaven's net. You know that whatever you send out will be what comes back to you some day. And as a DO scientist, you'll be on your way to becoming a Taoist master!

And even though those old Taoist masters were the ones who spoke the most clearly about this science of DO, nobody needs to change their religion to Taoism to benefit from studying DO. Understanding these principles can make an atheist a better atheist, a Baptist a better Baptist, a Hindu a better Hindu, or a Buddhist a better Buddhist because these laws are universal to all religion and all non-religion.

Whatever your beliefs, whatever your background, applying the laws of DO will bring you greater peace, greater understanding, and a more effective way to live.

Think right and happy practice!

PUBLISHER'S NOTE

If you'd like to learn more about practices like Taichi, Qigong, or Tao Gong, the Taichi Tao Center and Taichi Tao Productions offers several other books as well as a video library online where you can try these moving meditations for yourself.

If you want to experience the old traditional mouth-to-ear teaching, or as close as you can get in today's modern world, we have both live and recorded dialogues with our students who ask Master Waysun Liao their own deepest questions about their practice and life journey. Visit Taichitao.tv to follow along and discover how powerful mouth-to-ear teaching can be.

It's the twenty-first century and, unfortunately, that old temple system died out long ago. But thanks to technology, everybody can learn DO from a master without needing to move to or be accepted by a temple. We can preserve and recreate the authentic and powerful methods they used so that thousands can benefit from DO mouth-to-ear teaching in their own living rooms through the miracle of the internet. We invite you to keep your DO journey going by joining along with us and taking advantage of our many resources and materials.